Jesus Christ,
Word of the Father

Jesus Christ, Word of the Father

✠

THE SAVIOR OF THE WORLD

**Prepared by
The Theological-Historical Commission
for the Great Jubilee of the Year 2000**

*Translated from the Italian by
Adrian Walker*

A Crossroad Herder Book
The Crossroad Publishing Company
New York

Scripture quotations are from the Revised Standard Version,
Old Testament © 1952, New Testament © 1946 by the Division of
Christian Education of the National Council of the Churches of Christ
in the United States of America.

1997

The Crossroad Publishing Company
370 Lexington Avenue, New York, NY 10017

Original edition: *Cristo, Verbo del Padre:*
Gesù, unico Salvatore del mondo, ieri, oggi e sempre

Copyright © 1996 by Edizioni San Paolo (Milan)

English translation copyright © 1997 by
The Crossroad Publishing Company

Printed in the United States of America

Library of Congress Cataloging-in-Publication Data

Cristo, verbo del Padre. English.
    Jesus Christ, Word of the Father : the Savior of the world /
prepared under the direction of the Theological-Historical
Commission of the Great Jubilee of the Year 2000 ; translated from
the Italian by Adrian Walker.
        p. cm.
    "A Crossroad Herder book."
    Includes bibliographical references.
    ISBN 0-8245-1658-3 (pbk.)
    1. Jesus Christ – Person and offices. 2. Mary, Blessed Virgin,
Saint – Theology. 3. Spiritual life – Catholic Church. 4. Catholic
Church – Doctrines. I. Theological-Historical Commission of the
Great Jubilee of the Year 2000. II. Title.
BT202.C74813 1997
232 – dc21   96-48261
                                                       CIP

Contents

Abbreviations

AAS	*Acta Apostolicae Sedis,* Vatican City.
AG	*Ad Gentes:* Decree of the Second Vatican Council on the Church's missionary activity (1965)
CCC	*Catechism of the Catholic Church* (1992)
CT	*Catechesi Tradendae:* Apostolic Exhortation of John Paul II on catechesis (1965)
CTH	*Crossing the Threshold of Hope:* by John Paul II, ed. Vittorio Messori, trans. Jenny McPhee and Martha McPhee (New York: Alfred A. Knopf, 1994)
DM	*Dives in misericordia:* Encyclical Letter of John Paul II on God's mercy (1980)
DS	H. Denzinger-A. Schönmetzer, *Enchiridion symbolorum, definitionum et declarationum de rebus fidei et morum,* Freiburg in Br., 1965.
DV	*Dei Verbum:* Dogmatic Constitution of the Second Vatican Council on divine revelation (1965)
EN	*Evangelii Nuntiandi:* Apostolic Exhortation of Paul VI on evangelization in the modern world (1975)
EV	*Enchiridion Vaticanum,* Bologna, 1967–
EVi	*Evangelium Vitae:* Encyclical Letter of John Paul II on the value and inviolability of human life (1995)
GS	*Gaudium et Spes:* Pastoral Constitution of the Second Vatican Council on the Church in the modern world (1965)
LG	*Lumen Gentium:* Dogmatic Constitution of the Second Vatican Council on the Church (1964)
MC	*Marialis Cultus:* Apostolic Exhortation of Paul VI on veneration of the Blessed Virgin Mary
MD	*Mulieris Dignitatem:* Apostolic Letter of John Paul II on the dignity and vocation of woman (1988)

Puebla   Third General Conference of the Latin American
                Episcopate (1979)

RM   *Redemptoris Mater:* Encyclical Letter of John Paul II on
                the Blessed Virgin Mary in the life of the Church (1987)

RMi   *Redemptoris Missio:* Encyclical Letter of John Paul II on
                the permanent validity of the missionary mandate (1990)

Santo Domingo
                Fourth General Conference of the Latin American
                Episcopate (Santo Domingo, 1992)

SC   *Sacrosanctum Concilium:* Constitution of the Second
                Vatican Council on the liturgy (1963)

TM   *Testi Mariani del primo millenio:* Rome, 1988–91, I–IV

TMA   *Tertio Millennio Adveniente:* Apostolic Letter of John
                Paul II in preparation of the Jubilee of the Year
                2000 (1994)

VC   *Vita Consecrata:* postsynodal Apostolic Exhortation of
                John Paul II (1996)

VS   *Veritatis Splendor:* Encyclical Letter of John Paul II
                on some fundamental questions of the Church's moral
                teaching (1933)

WA   *Martin Luthers Werke. Kritische Gesamtausgabe,*
                Weimar, 1883–

Foreword

The approaching Jubilee of the year 2000 has a markedly christ-ological character: it is intended to be a celebration of the Incarnation of the Son of God, who enters into our history as the savior of humankind. No better and gladder tidings could be brought into the world. God, whose name could formerly not even be uttered, now shows himself to men and comes to share fully in our life.

In the prologue to his Gospel, Saint John the Evangelist describes this profound truth in the following words: "No one has ever seen God; the only Son, who is in the bosom of the Father, he has made him known" (Jn 1:18). The full revelation of the mystery of God begins in the person of Jesus of Nazareth. His actions and words, his silence and his glance give expression to the truth that man had always sought, but never found. The Second Vatican Council rightly taught that the mystery of every man's life, if it is not to be a mere puzzle, but to find meaning, has to be situated in the light of Christ. In revealing the mystery of the Father, Jesus reveals the meaning of the call to which each of us must respond in order to live in happiness and freedom from fear.

In his apostolic letter *Tertio Millennio Adveniente,* the Pope has underscored the special feature that has to characterize christological catechesis in this, the first of the preparatory years leading up to the Jubilee: "the rediscovery of Christ as Savior and Evangelizer." These two titles of Christ set forth in a new way the distinctiveness of our faith. The first is a call to revisit the mystery of salvation brought to fulfillment by the coming of Christ. Here we remember the deeply moving words of John the Evangelist: "For God sent the Son into the world, not to condemn the world, but that the world might be saved through him" (Jn 3:17). The second title confers new strength upon the mission of the Church, which was established by its Lord and Bridegroom to go out into the world announcing his resurrection to all the nations. It places before our eyes the model of every authentic evangelization: Jesus Christ himself, who is at one and the same time the content and the messenger of the Gospel.

This first year's catechesis will thus strive to impart a greater knowledge of the mystery of Christ, so that everyone may grow in faith and come to participate more intimately in this history of salvation. Flowing from this is the commitment — incumbent on every believer — to rehearse the stages of his baptism and to become increasingly aware of his responsibility to participate in the life of the Christian community. Baptism, which introduces us into the people of God, enables us to appropriate the gift of divine life and, in the words of the Apostle Paul, to "put on Christ" (Gal 3:27). Christian existence has a distinctive form because it is a life of faith, hope, and charity. It is, in other words, an existence that is capable of commitment in the present, but that looks toward the future which can fulfill every expectation of, and desire for, the good.

I entrust this valuable resource, which is the work of our Theological and Historical Commission, above all to the national committees, with the request that they assimilate it and mediate it in the various catechetical and pastoral initiatives planned for the year 1997. In addition, I am certain that all Christians wanting to have in hand a text for reflection and meditation, a text that offers solid knowledge of the mystery of Christ, will find this resource an invaluable contribution to the enrichment of their theological and cultural formation. I greet the publication of these texts, which are meant to be an official preparation for the catechesis that the Holy Father has desired for the three years leading up to the Jubilee, with my best wishes for its success. To these must be added hearty thanks to all those who have worked to make this endeavor a reality.

Cardinal ROGER ETCHEGARAY, President,
Organizing Committee for the Great Jubilee

Introduction

The present volume is an information and formation resource centered on the person of Jesus Christ, who is at the heart of the Jubilee of the year 2000. It is offered as an aid in preparing for the coming year 1997, which is dedicated to "reflection on Christ, the Word of the Father, who was made man by the work of the Holy Spirit" (*TMA*, 40).

It contains reasons for, and suggestions for reflection on, specific christological themes that we find indicated in *TMA* 40–43: the mystery of the Incarnation; the saving universality of Jesus, Savior and Evangelizer; the mystery of his birth from the Virgin Mary; the necessity of faith in Christ; the rediscovery of baptism; the valorization of catechesis as the teaching of the Apostles and the consequent necessity of a precise reference to the *Catechism of the Catholic Church;* the need to enlighten the consciences of the faithful about errors regarding the person of Christ; the longing for holiness and spiritual renewal; the presence of the Virgin Mary, the model of faith and the intimate associate in the saving mystery of Jesus.

All of this material is organized into ten chapters of varying lengths according to the following division. The first two chapters, which are introductory in nature, contain a reflection on the *mystery of the Incarnation* (chapter 1) and on the *rediscovery of catechesis* as the proclamation of the mystery of Christ and of his saving work (chapter 2).

The third chapter summarizes the *Christian understanding of Jesus Christ.* Particular emphasis is given to certain new models that are very close to our contemporary experience, such as the Christ of popular piety, the "contextual" or "inculturated" Christ, or the Christ of young people.

Chapters 4–9 contain some *catechetical-pastoral criteria* for a new, integral, and well-founded proclamation of the mystery of Christ to the people of God today.

These criteria are:

1. *The narration of the story of Jesus Christ* (chapters 4–7);

2. *the confession of Jesus, the Savior of all humanity* (chapter 8);

3. *the relevance of Christian salvation today* (chapter 9).

Chapter 10 focuses on the *presence of Mary* in the saving mystery of Christ. She is present as a merciful mother and as a model of faith, hope, and charity.

This study aid belongs to a special "genre." It is solely an introduction to the mystery of Jesus. Furthermore, the prose is conversational and invites the reader to become personally involved. Theological language is accompanied by catechetical reflections and pastoral suggestions. Reference to the Bible, which is always the basis of the book's reflections, is often broadened by reference to the Church's liturgical tradition, to popular piety, and to spirituality.

The present work, especially in chapters 5–7, is meant as an invitation to *retell the story of Jesus.* Chapter 5, for example, contains a summary of *Jesus' pedagogy;* Jesus welcomes the crowd of the poor and marginalized, he forgives and converts sinners, he heals the sick, honors women, welcomes the needy, defends the little ones and the weak, teaches forgiveness and love for one's enemies, reveals that the Father is rich in mercy, and faces his passion and death with courage. A concrete commitment for 1997 could be *to reread the Gospels in their entirety and, if possible, the whole New Testament, including the Book of Revelation.* The practice of *lectio divina* could aid in listening to and receiving the Word of God, and in this way could be a great stimulus to the renewal of the life of faith and of Christian witness in today's world.

The suggestions for pastoral ministry and spirituality found in the various chapters need, indeed, cannot do without, adaptation to the respective ecclesial and sociocultural contexts in which this work is read. In a word, we recommend taking a look around to rediscover the popular, musical, literary, symbolic, iconographic, architectural, and spiritual traditions of your own country and Church. Make the most of them and put new life into them in a creative way, as a gift to Jesus on the occasion of the great rendezvous of the third millennium of his saving Incarnation. A great help in doing this could be *the rediscovery and study of the evangelization of your own country and your own local or particular Church,* as well as knowledge of the concrete testimonies of charity and holiness that they offer.

It would be a good idea to pay greater attention to the discernment, to the purification, and to the catechetical and pastoral valorization of the manifestations of Christian *popular piety.* This popular piety consists of irreplaceable experiences of life in Christ on the part of the faithful. The main solemnities of the liturgical year, such as Christmas and Easter, are also the two major foci of the Christian people's heart-felt participation in salvation — in the joy of the birth and the resurrection and in the pain of the passion — by means of the sacraments of reconciliation and the Eucharist. Starting from these two essential nuclei of faith in Christ, you could try to rediscover in the context of your own local or particular Church the *christological expressions of popular piety:* adoration of the Blessed Sacrament, devotion to the Sacred Heart, Holy Week processions, pious exercises of the Via Crucis in Lent and of the Via Lucis in paschaltide.

Chapter 9 is devoted to setting forth four *orientations of our experience* of communion with Jesus Christ:

1. *The personal dimension of experience,* as the individual's rediscovery of his baptism;

2. *the communal dimension of experience,* that is, the experience of ecclesial communion;

3. *the experience of salvation,* as an experience of saved existence in Christ;

4. *the practical-cultural dimension of experience,* as the creation of a civilization of love.

This is an explicit call to inculturate Christianity. However, inculturation is seen here not just as a theory about how to transpose the Gospel conceptually into the various cultures of the world, but as a commitment on the part of all Christians to convert their hearts to the Gospel, in order to realize the work of the new evangelization and to bring to flower an authentic Christian culture re-created by the Holy Spirit.

Chapter 1

The Incarnation of the Son of God: The Center and the Fullness of Time and of History

The Proclamation of the "Acceptable Year"

The words spoken by Jesus at the beginning of his ministry in Nazareth continue to arouse joy, consolation, and boundless hope even today, at the end of the second millennium. Having entered the synagogue on the Sabbath day, Jesus stood up to read. He was handed the scroll of the prophet Isaiah:

> He opened the book and found the place where it was written, "The Spirit of the Lord is upon me, because he has anointed me to preach good news to the poor. He has sent me to proclaim release to the captives and recovering of sight to the blind, to set at liberty those who are oppressed, to proclaim the acceptable year of the Lord." And he closed the book, and gave it back to the attendant, and sat down; and the eyes of all in the synagogue were fixed on him. And he began to say to them, "Today this scripture has been fulfilled in your hearing." And all spoke well of him, and wondered at the gracious words which proceeded out of his mouth. (Lk 4:17–22)

The prophet Isaiah (see Is 61:1–2) had spoken of the Messiah. In Nazareth, Jesus exegetes Isaiah and affirms that the prophet's words find their fulfillment in him. Jesus is the promised Messiah who is consecrated by the Spirit of the Lord and sent to announce glad tidings: release to the captives, recovery of sight to the blind, freedom to the oppressed, an acceptable year of the Lord.

The intended purpose of the Jubilee of the year 2000 is to commemorate and relive the "acceptable year" that is inaugurated and realized in Jesus' person and work and is prolonged historically by the Church's witness. Twenty centuries have not only not dimmed the echo of this announcement, they have actually increased its attraction and its commanding urgency. Humankind, amazed at those words which even today still give light, strength, and courage to live, is turning its eyes back to the face of Jesus Christ.

The Jubilee is the commemoration of this life-giving event. It is not simply the recollection of a chronological date, but is above all the joyful and solemn remembrance of a reality: Jesus is permanently present in time and space to heal and save. This is the fulfillment and realization of God's good news for the poor of every era and nation.

In 1997, the Church invites Christians to reenact the Lord's prophetic gesture. Indeed, the celebration of the Jubilee year is a call to stand up, to take in hand the Gospel, and to read before all people the glad tidings of Jesus and to relive its message of joy, liberation, and grace with deep feeling, humility, courage, and creativity.

The Jubilee Is the Celebration of the Mystery of the Incarnation

Every year, the Church's liturgical calendar concentrates the central mysteries of the faith in two major celebrations: Christmas and Easter. In reality, there is just one saving event, the Incarnation of the Son of God, which begins with his birth in Bethlehem and comes to completion in his passion, death, and resurrection in Jerusalem. This is the bimillennial faith of the Church, which Christians reaffirm at Sunday Mass with the venerable words of the Creed:

I believe in one Lord, Jesus Christ,
the only Son of God,
eternally begotten of the Father...
through him all things were made.

For us men and for our salvation, he came down from
  heaven.
By the power of the Holy Spirit
he was born of the Virgin Mary
and became man.
For our sake he was crucified under Pontius Pilate.
He suffered, died, and was buried.
On the third day, he rose again from the dead in fulfillment
  of the Scriptures.
He ascended into heaven and is seated at the right hand of
  the Father.

Faith in the Incarnation of the Son of God is not the result
of human speculation at some later date. Nor does it have any
true parallels in other religions. It is a truth revealed by God, a
truth to which the Holy Scripture of the New Testament bears
unanimous witness.

Its most explicit linguistic formulation is found in the prologue of John's Gospel: "and the Word became flesh" (1:14).
The Greek term for flesh, *sarx*, is very close to the Hebrew
bâsâr; it denotes man as a fragile, transitory, mortal being. The
Word who was "with God" and "was God" (see Jn 1:1) thus
becomes true man — a visible, palpable, mortal being dwelling
in space and time.

The Pauline letters also make use of this terminology, which
suggests that the first Christian communities immediately considered and experienced the Incarnation to be a central truth of
their faith. In fact, for Saint Paul the Son of God "was descended
from David according to the flesh" (Rom 1:3); "of their [the
Israelites'] race according to the flesh, is the Christ" (Rom 9:5).
Indeed, the great mystery of our religion is the fact that Christ
"was manifested in the flesh" (1 Tim 3:16). For this reason, in
Christ "the whole fulness of deity dwells bodily" (Col 2:9).

A famous Pauline hymn — which many consider to be
pre-Pauline, hence, to antedate the year 50 — celebrates the
Incarnation as nothing less than a process of abasement and
humiliation to the point of annihilation through death on the
cross:

Christ Jesus...though he was in the form of God,
did not count equality with God
a thing to be grasped,
but emptied himself,
taking the form of a servant,
being born in the likeness of men.
And being found in human form he humbled himself
and became obedient unto death,
even death on a cross. (Phil 2:6–8)

For Saint Paul, the Incarnation is the mystery par excellence. It is "the mystery hidden for ages and generations, but now made manifest to his saints" (Col 1:26; see Eph 1:9; 3:3–5; 6:19). These saints, rooted and founded in love, "have power to comprehend...what is the breadth and length and height and depth" (Eph 3:18) of the saving plan of God's love in Christ. In another passage, Paul says that "when the time had fully come, God sent forth his Son, born of woman, born under the law, to redeem those who were under the law, so that we might receive adoption as sons" (Gal 4:4). The Incarnation is the mystery which the Father "set forth in Christ as a plan for the fulness of time, to recapitulate all things in him, things in heaven and things on earth" (Eph 1:9–10).

The Incarnation, as a plan that matured in the heart of the trinitarian communion, is a gift from on high. This is the teaching of Saint John, who affirms that "God so loved the world, that he gave his only Son, that whoever believes in him should not perish, but have eternal life" (Jn 3:16; see Jn 3:17; 10:36; 17:18; 1 Jn 4:9). The testimonies of Paul and John, which come at the beginning and at the end of the New Testament, respectively, are different voices in a symphony that converges in a single hymn of praise to the Lord Jesus, the incarnate Son of God.

The Incarnation is more than a major theoretical truth of Christianity. The affirmation that Jesus is true God and true man indicates the source of his power to save in history. The Incarnation has a "soteriological motive," which we find clearly stated already in the Nicene Creed: "for us men and for our

salvation, he came down from heaven and became man. He suffered, rose on the third day, and ascended into heaven. He will
come to judge the living and the dead" (DS, 125).

The doctrine of the Incarnation has been continually opposed
throughout history. Even in our day, some have regarded it as
a myth — the myth of the man Jesus, in whom, so it is said,
God manifested his saving presence in a particularly powerful
way. This interpretation amounts to a denial that Jesus Christ is
really true God and true man.

Contrary to these hypotheses, the mystery of the Incarnation
is the central point of the biblical witness and of the Christian
creed. Throughout its two-thousand-year history, the Church's
tradition has never ceased defending the Incarnation and giving
reasons for its credibility. The martyrs past and present have
not spared even their lives in order to attest to their profession
of faith in Jesus Christ, their Savior.

Consequently, the Incarnation is the unsurpassable height
and the absolute fulfillment of salvation history. Jesus Christ is
God's final and definitive word to humankind (Heb 1:2), the
sole mediator between God and men (1 Tim 2:5; see Heb 8:6;
9:15; 12:24), the source of all salvation, both now and in the
future (see Acts 4:12).

The Incarnation reveals the mystery of God's intratrinitarian
life, the mystery of the participation of man and the cosmos in
the glory of God, and the mystery of the Church as the prolon-
gation in history of the coming of the kingdom (see Mt 13:38;
16:18-19; 21:43; 22:1-14; Heb 12:28). "The mystery of the Incarnation of the Word has the force of all the secrets and figures
of Scripture and the knowledge of all creatures, both visible and
invisible" (Maximus the Confessor, *Capita theologica et oeco-
nomica*, 66). This is why "only the incarnate Word can teach
us the knowledge of God" (Maximus the Confessor, *Orationis
dominicae expositio*).

The Incarnation as the "Fulness of Time"

The crowded stage of world history has seen enlightened and
wise monarchs, courageous and daring commanders, and pro-

found and extraordinarily gifted thinkers in various fields of human knowledge succeed one another in space and time. In every people we find figures who have ennobled their own land, indeed, all of humanity. But no one has marked the history of the world as greatly as Jesus of Nazareth. His preaching lasted no more than three years. But it set the world on fire. The mystery of his death and resurrection brought the hope of endless life into history.

History has been given its true fulness: "The fulness of time is one and the same as the mystery of the Incarnation of the Word, the consubstantial Son of the Father, and as the mystery of the world's redemption" (TMA, 1). Even Luther, in his commentary on Gal 4:4 — "when the time had fully come, God sent his Son" — rightly explains that "it was not so much time that caused the Son to be sent, as it was the sending of the Son that created the time of fulness" (WA, 57, 30.15).

A quick survey of human history at the time of Jesus' birth reveals that the ancient world had had a wide and various religious preparation. The great Hindu and Buddhist traditions, which were not entirely unknown in the Mediterranean world at that time, had dominated the Far East for centuries. In the Middle East and the West, not only did each people have its own traditional forms of religion, but the pagan religions of Greco-Roman origin were booming, often because they were imposed on conquered peoples by force of arms. The Hebrew religion, as old as the Hindu tradition, flourished in an obscure corner of the Roman Empire. It was this religion that served as the proximate preparation for the coming of Jesus: "In fact, the economy of the Old Testament is essentially ordered to prepare the coming of Christ, the Redeemer of the world, and the inauguration of his messianic kingdom" (TMA, 6).

A dynamic movement toward the saving Incarnation runs mightily throughout the Old Testament, both in the history of the chosen people and in the figures of messianic mediators such as kings, prophets, and priests. However, it must be pointed out, for the sake of exactness, that by the time of Christ this dynamism had entered a period of great confusion. The decisive initial period stretched from the vocation of Abraham (nineteenth centuries B.C.) to the Exodus and God's covenant with the people (thirteenth century B.C.), and was followed by the glorious events of the Davidic and Solomonic monarchy (eleventh–tenth century B.C.). But the division of the kingdom (tenth century) and the Babylonian exile (sixth century) began a history of failures that culminated in political and religious subjection, first to the Persians (538–333 B.C.), then to the Greeks (333–63 B.C.), and finally to the Romans. By the time of the Roman occupation under Pompey in 63 B.C., all of the chosen people's mediations of salvation had failed before God and history.

The downfall of the traditions and institutions that sustained Israel had encouraged a novel hope in an eschatological Messiah. Isaiah puts it like this: "Thus says the Lord.... Remember not the former things, nor consider the things of old. Behold I am doing a new thing" (Is 43:16; 18–19). The change from the failure of the old to the hope of the new is a "transition without transition." In other words, it does not occur on account of the extreme gravity of the situation. Rather, it happens by God's intervention. This intervention bursts forth with absolute newness at the nadir of history, in order to introduce into history God's definitive salvation and to open it to all humankind.

The passage from the Old to the New Testament cannot be located on the horizontal line of a homogeneous evolution. It is a qualitative leap from on high. This qualitative leap occurs in the birth of Jesus Christ: "The true origin of Jesus cannot be found in this world; it is hidden in eternity" (Augustine, *De Trinitate,* 4, 20, 29).

This is the burden of the opening lines of the Letter to the Hebrews:

> In many and various ways God spoke of old to our Fathers by the prophets; but in these last days he has spoken to us by a Son, whom he appointed the heir of all things, through whom he also created the world. (Heb 1:1–2)

The event of Christ was not the outcome of time and of the urgent expectation of the Messiah. Rather, it was the Incarnation of the Son of God, the gratuitous gift of the triune God, that gave time its authentic saving "fulness."

Only with the Incarnation of the Son of God does history enter into a phase of worldwide, universal salvation. Only with the Incarnation do all the nations that had been dispersed at Babel receive the call to participate in the Spirit of the risen Christ on the day of Pentecost. The Incarnation is what makes Christianity something new. For Jesus is not a prophet who speaks in the name of God, but is God himself speaking and saving: "He is God who comes in Person to speak of himself to man and to show him the way by which to reach him" (*TMA*, 6).

The Incarnation as God's "Becoming"

An appropriate way to continue our meditation is to reflect on the paradoxical fact that God *becomes:* "In Jesus Christ, the incarnate Word, time becomes a dimension of God, who in himself is eternal" (*TMA*, 10). This is a statement of a reality specific to Christianity. Through the Incarnation of the Son of God, time is assumed by the second Person of the Most Holy Trinity, who, while remaining God, also becomes perfect man. The Council of Chalcedon professes that Jesus Christ is

> perfect in his divinity and perfect in his humanity, true God and true man..., consubstantial with the Father by the divinity and consubstantial with us by the humanity..., generated by the Father before all ages according to the divinity, and in these latter days, for us men and for our salvation, by Mary, virgin and mother of God, according to the humanity. (DS, 301)

In Holy Scripture, the living God transcends time and things: "Before the mountains were brought forth, or ever thou hadst formed the earth and the world, from everlasting to everlasting, thou art God" (Ps 90:2).

He is immutable: "Of old thou didst lay the foundations of the earth, and the heavens are the work of thy hands. They will perish, but thou dost endure. Thou changest them like raiment, and they pass away; but thou art the same, and thy years have no end" (Ps 102:26–28).

The oracle of Malachi says: "I the Lord do not change" (Mal 3:6).

The New Testament likewise speaks of the "Father of lights with whom there is no variation or shadow due to change" (Jas 1:17). Jesus, speaking of himself, says "before Abraham was, I am" (Jn 8:58; 13:19). Indeed, the Word "was in the beginning with God" (Jn 1:2).

The preexistence, the eternity, and the immutability of God are fundamentally biblical, rather than philosophical, items. Hence those propositions that define the Church's faith that God is "eternal and immutable" (see the creed of the Fourth Lateran Council [1215]: DS, 800).

The reality of the eternity and immutability of God reaches its peak of paradoxicality in the Incarnation of the Son of God. Saint John's prologue strikingly brings out the contrast. The Word, while eternal and preexistent (see Jn 1:1–3), "became flesh" (Jn 1:14), was "born of woman" (Gal 4:4). He thus became a spatio-temporal reality that experiences growth (see Lk 2:52) and mortality. While God is truly eternal, he just as truly becomes man, which is to say, space, time, history. Consequently, human history also becomes God's history, and man's death becomes part of the experience of the incarnate Son of God.

In order to understand better God's becoming, it is necessary to be clear about the meaning of the affirmation. God, *the* living one par excellence, freely unfolds his superabundant vitality both in creation and redemption, without therefore losing in perfection. In his infinite exuberance of life, God can burst forth freely in the time and space of his creation. In this regard, he is different from his creatures, because for them becoming is a necessity inherent in what they are. Creatures cannot not become. Indeed, this ineluctable becoming is the primary condition of their development and existence. Creatures are in becoming because they are themselves becoming. By contrast, God's becoming is absolute liberty and gratuity that flows forth from his free and loving choice. This is why God's becoming not only does not involve imperfection, but even becomes the highest principle by which humankind is remade into a new creature.

On the other hand, the creation itself is already a prelude to God's free becoming in history. In man, created in the image and likeness of God, God had already made a "sketch" of what any free self-manifestation of his in history would look like. He thus prepared a "way" for his free in-breaking into time and space. The Incarnation of the Word is this supreme fulfillment of humanity. The humanity of the Word, in its creaturely integrity, arrives in God, thus reaching its full realization.

Inasmuch as the divine life is the immanent support of every time, indeed, its eternal present, the risen Christ is not only able to interfere with time, but he is progressively manifested and understood in time. This happens through the resurrection, the ascension, Pentecost, and the life of the Church. "With the coming of Christ, the 'last days' (Heb 1:2), the 'last hour' (1 Jn 2:18) begin; this is the beginning of the time of the Church, which will last until the Parousia" (*TMA,* 10). The Church continues in time the pedagogy of revealing and communicating Jesus' "proexistence," his existence "for us."

Christ: The "Center" of Time

In the New Testament, time is always seen in relation to Christ, who is its center. Hence the division of history into two sections coming, respectively, before and after Christ. The Christian calendar does not reckon the years from an initial point — from creation, as does the Hebrew calendar — but from a central point, that is, the birth of Jesus. The historical fact of the Incarnation is the center of history: from this event history is dated backward and forward. The coming of Christ is the temporal center of everything that happens in history.

This, then, is the Christian conception of time. It is not a question of a mere historical convention, but of a theological criterion: the coming of Christ is the center of history because it gives history its meaning and its saving efficacy. All historical events, whether before or after Christ, are related to Christ and are evaluated in the light of the work and person of Christ, who introduces his grace into history. Time thus becomes a condition of the possibility of salvation for humankind and the cosmos. Considered in relation to the Incarnation, world history ceases to be profane and becomes sacred history. This christocentric perspective places on the same temporal line both God's initial creation and the eschatological arrival of human history and all natural events in God, both the historical events of the people of Israel and the acts of Jesus, his Apostles, and the Church.

Unlike other religions, in which time is antithetical to God and salvation, Christianity values time as the means which God uses to become incarnate and to reveal and give his grace. Christianity does not conceive of time as a cyclical repetition and salvation as exodus from time. Rather, in Christianity time takes a linear form. This suggests that time and salvation are destined to meet in history, which thereby becomes salvation history.

On this time line, Christ's paschal mystery is the redemptive event par excellence. Easter is like the decisive battle of a war that is still to end. Even though in history the hostilities continue and not everyone has acknowledged the definitive import of that battle, it nevertheless already signals victory. The cross and the resurrection are the decisive battle that has already won the war. The crowning moment of history is the resurrection of Jesus. The appropriation of the grace of Christ takes place within history as it tends toward the end of time. Hope in the future therefore becomes even more intense, based as it is on the conviction that the decisive victory has already been gained — that victory which is the foundation and the first fruits of the salvation of the whole world.

Time draws its life from this centrality of Christ. It becomes the line of Christ, who is before every time, who died yesterday in Palestine, who lives today as the risen one, and who will return as judge at the end of time. The times of history — past, present, and future — are what they are in reference to Jesus, who "is the same yesterday and today and forever" (Heb 13:8).

The historical-chronological background of the New Testament is thus essentially christological. Matthew presents Jesus' earthly life as the fulfillment of the history of Israel. For Luke, Jesus is the center of time and of salvation history. In the Apocalypse, Jesus is the beginning and the end, the Alpha and the Omega (see Rev 21:6).

Concretely, the New Testament sees history consisting in a double movement. The first movement is one of contraction; it starts from the creation of humankind and arrives via the chosen people at Christ, the only Savior. The second movement, which is one of expansion, starts from Christ and extends via the Church to the whole of humanity. Our history exists within this movement of expansion, which extends to all the peoples saved by and in Christ. We live in the time of the Church, which extends from the resurrection to the Parousia. The Church, as the center of the earth, manifests visibly the sovereignty of Christ in human history. By the celebration of the Eucharist, the synthesis and the summit of its sacramental action, and by the preaching of the Gospel, the Church gives to the present time its full significance as salvation history.

Chapter 2

"The Rediscovery of Catechesis" as the Proclamation of the Person of Jesus Christ and of His Saving Mystery (*TMA,* 42)

The Catechesis of Jesus, the First and Perfect Evangelizer

Jesus was a great evangelizer. He proclaimed the good news that God's kingdom was coming in his person, and he did so with the enthusiasm, the conviction, and the authority of an unsurpassable teacher. "And Jesus went about all the cities and villages, teaching in their synagogues and preaching the Gospel of the kingdom, and healing every disease and every infirmity" (Mt 9:35; see also 4:23 and Mk 6:34).

Saint Luke's Gospel presents a day of Jesus' apostolate in the Galilean city of Capernaum (see Lk 4:31–44). It is a string of teachings, miracles, changes of scene, acts of hospitality. For Jesus, after having taught the people, cures in the synagogue a man afflicted by an unclean spirit. At Simon's house, he heals Peter's mother-in-law, who lay abed with a great fever. In the evening he heals a multitude of sick people suffering from every kind of disease. Early in the morning of the following day, while he was in a place apart, he was met by a large crowd that wanted to detain him in the area. But Jesus departed Capernaum for other cities, "and he was preaching in the synagogues of Judea" (Lk 4:44). No less than twice the Evangelist underscores the people's amazement at the authority and power manifested by Jesus' words and works: "they were astonished at his teaching, for his word was with authority" (see Lk 4:32, 36).

Looked at as a whole, Jesus' evangelization is a "comprehensive" form of communication. First, he taught with language, using a variety of literary genres, such as short discourses, parables, aphorisms, similes, and words illustrated by deeds. Some of the unforgettable moments of this teaching are, among others, the Sermon on the Mount — a programmatic statement of the nature of Christianity (Mt 5–7) — which begins with the unsettling Beatitudes (Mt 5:3–12); the parables of the Good Samaritan (Lk 10:30–37) and the Prodigal Son (Lk 15:11–32); the discourse on the last judgment (Mt 25:31–46); the great instruction which Jesus gives to his disciples at the Last Supper (Jn 13–17).

Jesus' way of acting was also an important communication tool. He evangelized by certain unconventional attitudes toward the poor, the marginalized, the sick, the needy, enemies, foreigners, women, children, and the law and the temple, attitudes that did not conform to the religious and social culture of the time.

Furthermore, he communicated by means of a great number of miracles of every kind, miracles which became signs of his divine power as well as of God's provident presence in history. The miracles aroused amazement and eagerness to receive Jesus, but also stirred up jealousy and hatred. For disciples and enemies alike, the miracles were an opportunity to understand Jesus and to pass from acceptance of his prophetic authority (*exousía*) to the question of his divine reality (*ousía*), from his extraordinary power to his extraordinary being.

Jesus communicated with his actions, his silences, his gaze. Even his locomotion became a communication of salvation. His journey to Jerusalem had a precise purpose: to reveal and accomplish his redemptive mission: "Behold, we are going up to Jerusalem; and the Son of man will be delivered to the chief priests and scribes, and they will deliver him to the gentiles to be mocked and scourged and crucified, and he will be raised on the third day" (Mt 20:18–19).

The disciples' call to follow Jesus (see Mk 1:16–20) was itself a communication of extraordinary religious truths, as well as an experience of sharing in the Jesus' life and apostolic ideals. The disciples' following involved daily communion "with him"

(Mk 3:14; "they stayed with him," Jn 1:39) in preaching, in prayer, in the joy of the prodigious miracles (the miracle of the changing of water into wine during the wedding at Cana: Jn 2:2–11), in the intimacy of the Last Supper (Jn 13–17), and in Jesus' sorrow over the death of Lazarus (Jn 11), the imminent passion (Jn 18), and the crucifixion (Jn 19:26–27). The life and mission of Jesus became the life and mission of the disciples.

The paschal mystery of death and resurrection was the utmost sealing of Jesus' total communication. This mystery is continued in history not only in the preaching of the disciples, but above all in the sacrament of the Eucharist, which brings about in time and space the interpersonal encounter of every believer with Jesus the Evangelizer and Savior.

In the three years of his public life, Jesus carried out an education in faith so total in its scope that it became an out and out vital osmosis. Through this intense pedagogy, which reached its greatest density and maturity in Easter, Jesus communicated and grounded the two essential nuclei of the Christian faith: (1) we attain salvation not so much by applying the law, but by faith in his person and event (that is, the event of Christ as the personal starting-point of Christian faith); (2) Christian salvation reaches its high point when it becomes a vital experience of relationship with God the Father, Son, and Holy Spirit (that is, the trinitarian communion as the mature personal end-point of Christian existence).

Jesus' teaching thus had a strong christocentric and trinitarian streak. Jesus showed that Christian salvation is a concrete life of personal interrelation with God. The Gospel of Saint John forcefully depicts this catechetical journey of maturation, a journey that begins with faith in Christ and arrives at life in the Father, the Son, and the Holy Spirit: "If a man loves me, he will keep my word, and my Father will love him, and we will come to him and make our home with him" (Jn 14:23).

The First Christian Proclamation: Jesus Is "Lord"

Even before Easter, Jesus had promised Peter the "power of the keys" ("I will give you the keys to the kingdom of heaven,"

Mt 16:19), which included the task of teaching with authority. However, it was after the paschal event (death-resurrection-ascension-Pentecost) that the Apostles and disciples, acting with extraordinary effectiveness and dedication, made themselves living echoes of their master's saving proclamation (hence the term *catechesis*, from the Greek *katechéo*, which means "I let ring out, I teach *viva voce*). Saint Paul, for example, says, "Let *him who is catechized* in the word share all good things with *him who catechizes*" (Gal 6:6; the verb is used twice). The teaching of the Lord Jesus, together with his death and resurrection, becomes the content of the preaching of the first Christian missionaries and the substance of the first Christian writings. For this reason, the Gospels are nothing but the first great catechisms of the primitive Christian communities (see Lk 1:4). In his Letter to the Romans, Paul says that "if you confess with your lips that Jesus is Lord...you will be saved" (Rom 10:9; see 1 Cor 12:3; Phil 2:11).

Some see 1 Cor 15:3–5, where Paul reminds the Corinthians of the essential core of the *depositum fidei* that he had received and transmitted, as a first *written summary of postpaschal catechesis*. "For I delivered to you as of first importance what I also received, that Christ died for our sins in accordance with the scriptures, that he was buried, that he was raised on the third day in accordance with the scriptures, and that he appeared to Cephas, then to the twelve." The basic instruction of Christians was the proclamation of the death, burial, and resurrection of Jesus and of the appearances of the Risen One.

Discipleship is not just proclamation and faith. After Easter, it becomes both testimony to Jesus (to the point of martyrdom) and a life of communion with the Father, with the risen Son, and with the Holy Spirit in a life of brotherhood in the Church. The Pauline and Johannine letters reveal something of the great christological and trinitarian focus of the faith of the first Christian communities: "we are the temple of the living God" (2 Cor 6:16) because we are called to communion with the Holy Spirit (see 2 Cor 13:13; Phil 2:1) and "with the Father and with his Son Jesus Christ" (1 Jn 1:3; 6–7; 1 Cor 1:9; 6:15, 19). The core of the catechesis of Jesus and about Jesus is education and maturation of faith in the person of Christ, such faith being a life of salvation in the communion of the Trinity.

Post-Easter catechesis is thus also understood and experienced as a maturation and a comprehensive communication of faith through the proclamation of Jesus (*kérygma*), the prayer and sacramental action of the Church (*leiturgía, eucharistía*), service to the needy (*diakonía*), communion with God and the brethren (*koinonía, ekklesía*), and testimony, even the supreme testimony of martyrdom (*martyría*). In this way, post-Easter catechesis, like that of Jesus, is comprehensive. Furthermore, it is *essential*, inasmuch as it centers on faith in the mystery of the Trinity, and *integral*, insofar as it takes hold of the entire existence of persons and communities in their historical existence and in the perspective of the eschaton. It is essentially this structure that we find in the *Catechism of the Catholic Church* published in 1992. The *Catechism* is divided into four parts. The first part is an in-depth presentation of the profession of faith, that is, the *Creed*. The second part instructs the reader in the liturgical and sacramental *celebration* of the Christian mystery. The third part contains Jesus' and the Church's teaching on the *moral life* and on the commandments. The final part offers formation in the life of *prayer;* it includes a full catechesis on the *Our Father*. And Jesus Christ is the teacher who illuminates and sustains these four dimensions of the one Christian existence. He is, in fact, the object of the true faith; he is present with his saving action in the Church and in its sacraments; he is the model, source, and support (with his grace) of Christian action; he is the teacher and inspiration, together with the Holy Spirit, of our prayer to the Father.

Jesus Christ: Center of the Church's Catechesis

The call to return to Jesus Christ as the authentic center and source of the Christian message emerged explicitly in the Second Vatican Council, which Paul VI called "the great catechism of modern times" (*AAS,* 58 [1966], p. 575). In the inaugural discourse of the Council (11 November 1962), John XXIII placed Jesus Christ "at the center of history and life; men are either with him and his Church, in which case they enjoy light, goodness, order, and peace, or else they are without him" (*EV,* 1, 31).

Christocentrism is one of the most powerful keys to the interpretation of Vatican II. This is true whether we take the first document — "Christ is always present in his Church, and in a special way in the liturgical celebrations" (*SC,* 7) — or the Dogmatic Constitution on Divine Revelation — "Christ the Lord, in whom the whole revelation of the Most High God is completed" (*DV,* 7) — or the last document, which affirms in paragraph 22:

> In reality, the mystery of man is illuminated only in the mystery of the incarnate Word. For Adam, the first man, was a figure of the one to come, that is, of Christ the Lord. Christ, who is the new Adam, in the very revelation of the mystery of the Father and of his love, also fully reveals man to man and makes known to him his exalted vocation.... Through Christ and in Christ light is shed on that enigma of suffering and death which oppresses us apart from the Gospel. Christ is risen, destroying death by his death, and he has given us life, so that, sons in the Son, we can cry out in the Spirit, "Abba! Father!" (*GS,* 22)

The recovery of christocentrism in evangelization and in catechesis implies the reaffirmation of the centrality of Jesus Christ in the proclamation of faith as a path of maturation, education, and formation of Christian existence in its concreteness and comprehensiveness. This is, in fact, the definition of catechesis:

> The name "catechesis" was given to the ensemble of efforts undertaken in the Church to make disciples, to help men believe that Jesus is the Son of God so that, through faith, they may have life in his name, and to educate and instruct them in this life and build up the body of Christ. (*CT,* 1)

Christocentrism in catechesis has a twofold function. First of all, it indicates that Jesus Christ is the only true teacher, which is why in catechesis we must teach only the doctrine and life of

Jesus (*CT,* 6–8). In the second place, catechesis places at the center of its message the very "person" of the Savior, his mystery of Incarnation, suffering, death, and redemptive resurrection. In fact, the ultimate goal of catechesis is "to put someone not only in contact, but in communion with Jesus Christ: he alone can lead to the love of the Father in the Spirit and can let us participate in the life of the Holy Trinity" (*CT,* 5).

The Christocentric Inspiration of the Jubilee of the Year 2000

This return to christocentrism is nothing but a return to the authentic element of the Christian message. For the event of Christ, the understanding of his mystery, and the sharing of his discipleship is the locus of the revelation of the authentic name of God and of the significance and value of the saved existence of every human person.

Insistence on the proclamation of Jesus Christ is the central theme of John Paul II's 1990 encyclical *Redemptoris Missio,* as well as of the document *Dialogo e Annuncio* (Dialogue and Proclamation, 1991) of the Pontifical Council for Interreligious Dialogue and the Congregation for the Evangelization of the Peoples.

The final document of the Fourth General Conference of the Latin American Episcopate (Santo Domingo, 1992), has an intrinsically christocentric structure. The bishops affirm the following: "We proclaim our faith and our love for Jesus Christ. He is the same 'yesterday and today and forever' (see Heb 13:8)." The three parts of the document are also christological: (1) Jesus Christ, Gospel of the Father; (2) Jesus Christ, Evangelizer Living in His Church; (3) Jesus Christ, Life and Hope of Latin America.

John Paul II's moral encyclical *Veritatis Splendor* (1993) also has a christocentric structure. "Jesus Christ is the true light that enlightens every man" (see introduction, 1–4), and he is the true teacher of moral action for the whole of humanity. Every human being addresses to him today the question of the rich young man: "Master, what must I do to gain eternal life?" (see

1, 6–27). The same must be said for John Paul II's second moral encyclical, *Evangelium vitae* (1995), which is centered entirely on Jesus Christ, the life and life-giver of humanity and the cosmos. John Paul II's christocentrism brings Christian morality back to its original source, and in this way spurs us on to the filial dynamism of an assimilation to Christ in obedience to the Father. The horizon of man's being and action is, in fact, the reality of the Incarnation of the Son of God.

The Pope sets forth this total reference to Jesus Christ once again in the postsynodal exhortation *Vita Consecrata* (1996). The consecrated life is a life centered on the unique value that is the person of Jesus. It makes visible the earthly existence of Jesus Christ in the history of humanity: "With the profession of the evangelical counsels, *the characteristic features of Jesus — virginal, poor, and obedient — acquire a typical and permanent 'visibility' in the midst of the world*" (VC, 1).

The apostolic letter *Tertio Millennio Adveniente* (1994) reflects this context of the rediscovery of the centrality of Christ in catechesis and evangelization: Christ is "the only mediator between God and man" (*TMA*, 4); he is "Lord of the cosmos and of history" (see *TMA*, 5); he is "the Lord of time, its beginning and its consummation" (*TMA*, 10).

The Jubilee, as the suitable time for reevangelization and for the maturation of faith, must be animated by this inner christological reality, which is essentially trinitarian: "The ideal structure for this triennium, which is centered on Christ, the Son of God made man, can only be theological, that is, trinitarian" (*TMA*, 39). The center of reflection will be the deepening appreciation of "Jesus Christ, the only savior of the world, yesterday and today and forever" (*TMA*, 40).

And the year 1997, which marks the beginning of the triennium in preparation for the year 2000, is "dedicated to reflection on Christ, the Word of the Father, who became man by the working of the Holy Spirit. It is, in fact, necessary to underscore the markedly christological character of the Jubilee, which will celebrate the Incarnation of the Son of God, the mystery of salvation for the whole human race" (*TMA*, 40).

Chapter 3

Being "Christian": Jesus Christ in the Understanding of Contemporary Christians

"But Who Do You Say That I Am?" (Mt 16:15)

On 15 August 1988, the international review *Time Magazine* put the face of Jesus on its cover for the sixteenth time. The artist, Rudy Hoglund, had created a portrait of Jesus composed of a "mosaic" of twenty-nine tesserae. These tesserae were details of seventeen famous images of Christ painted throughout history: mosaics, icons, frescoes, stained glass, etchings, tapestries, and paintings ancient and modern. Although produced in different periods of history by different artists using different techniques, the small tesserae, suitably arranged, produced a face that was "recognizably" Jesus'. A sort of continuity of content in the discontinuity of forms. Despite the different interpretations of Jesus that have been given both inside and outside Christianity, what the Letter to the Hebrews says about him remains true: "Jesus Christ is the same yesterday and today and forever" (Heb 13:8).

The Christ of theology, of pastoral work, and of Christian evangelization is not only an exemplary model of humanity, nor simply an inspired prophet of God's will and law among men. In other words, Jesus does not merely teach us to be men or to be men of faith. He invites us to be "his own": "Abide in me, and I in you.... I am the vine, you are the branches" (Jn 15:4–5). This implies the living acknowledgment of Jesus as "Lord and Christ" (Acts 2:36), as the savior of all humankind (Acts 4:12), as the only revealer and mediator between God and men (see 1 Tim 2:5–6).

For the primitive community, to call oneself "Christian" (see

37

Acts 11:26) meant to accept Christ as the horizon and the definitive support of all of humankind's hopes for salvation; it meant
to see in him the one who reconciles all things (Col 1:20; Eph
1:10), the one who liberates from slavery to evil (Rom 6:17–
18), the one who re-creates man (Rom 5:1; Tit 3:5–6), and the
incarnate Son of God (Jn 1:14) who was profoundly man while
being truly the Son of God (see Heb 2:17–18; 4:14–15; 5:7–8).
The Christian understanding of Jesus surpasses and fulfills religious and humanistic interpretations of him. For Christians,
Jesus is not a relative value, that is, one of the many great
models of humanity and religiosity, but an absolute value. For
Christians, he and he alone can bring every human person,
together with the whole of humanity and the cosmos, to full
realization.

The following text of Paul VI is a model statement about
Jesus:

> Jesus is at the summit of human aspirations,
> the end of our hopes and our prayers,
> the focal point of the desires of history and civilization;
> he is the Messiah, the center of humanity,
> he who gives value to every human action,
> who is the joy and the plenitude of the desires of all hearts;
> he is the true man, the type of perfection, beauty, holiness
> whom God has set up to embody the true model,
> the true concept of man; he is the brother of all,
> the irreplaceable friend,
> the only one worthy of all confidence and love:
> he is the Christ-man.
> And at the same time Jesus is at the source
> of all of our true happiness,
> his is the light by which the space of the world
> takes on proportions, form, beauty, and shadow;
> he is the word that defines everything, explains everything,
> classifies everything, redeems everything;
> he is the principle of our spiritual and moral life;
> he tells us what we must do and he gives us the strength,
>   the grace to do it;

his image, indeed, his presence reverberates
in every soul that makes itself a mirror
to receive the ray of his truth and life,
who believes in him
and welcomes his sacramental contact;
he is Christ-God, the Master, the Savior, the Life."
(Allocution of 3 February 1964)

While the central core of the proclamation of Christ has re-
mained unchanged, from the very beginning Christians have
used various interpretive "models" of the event of Christ.
Rather than a complete inventory of two thousand years of
Christian history, we give here a simple map of the major
perspectives of contemporary christology, both Catholic and
non-Catholic.

The Glorious Christ of the Orthodox Tradition

It is not reinterpretation of Jesus in terms of inculturation, nor
the aspiration to praxis that gives Eastern Orthodox christology
its distinctive note, but serene possession of faith in Christ and
participation in his divinity (i.e., divinization) through continual
praise in liturgy, asceticism, contemplation, and illumination.
Orthodox christology finds its starting-point in the Johannine
affirmation that the Son of God becomes flesh (see Jn 1:14). The
Incarnation is considered as the event that decides the destiny
of the cosmos, that reestablishes and renews creation, restoring
to the universe and to man their original divine glory. In this
context, the Orthodox affirm with conviction that man attains
authentic realization when he participates in the life of God.

In methodological terms, Orthodox christology is worked
out and understood within the tradition of the Fathers and the
early Councils. Assuming that this ecclesial tradition is essentially definitive and sufficient, the Orthodox emphasize without
doubts and hesitations the divine glory of Jesus, true man and
true God, whom they almost always called *Theós Lógos* (God
the Word).

Orthodox catechesis is also essentially christological. Relating this catechesis to the icons, the Orthodox understand it as a contemplation of the "iconostasis," that is, of the major feasts of the Church's liturgy, which keep time to the mysteries of the earthly and the glorified Christ: the birth of Jesus, his baptism, the transfiguration, the preaching of the kingdom, the cross and resurrection, the ascension and Pentecost, his second coming. The narration of the mysteries of the life of Jesus occurs in the context of the Church's tradition, without too much distraction or too many concessions to the challenges of today's irreligion and indifference.

The Crucified Christ of the Lutheran Vision

For Luther, the only perspective from which we can understand and proclaim Christ is the theology of the cross, which is the synthesis of the entire Christian message. "The Word of the cross" (see 1 Cor 1:18) is not only the fact of Jesus' passion and death, but also a model for interpreting the entirety of Christian revelation: "In Christ crucified is the true theology and the true knowledge of God" (*WA*, 1, 262). The cross is the problematic and provocative identity of true Christian identity. The crucified God is the true criterion of every Church, of every theology, and of the whole truth of Christianity.

The Richness of the Catholic Christological Vision

The Catholic vision, both in systematic reflection or in catechetical and pastoral transmission, is characterized:

1. by its emphasis on the humanity of Jesus, which is seen both as leading to the discovery and affirmation of his divinity and as the model of full human realization;

2. by dialogue with the contemporary world, which gives rise to a multiplicity of interpretive approaches to the mystery of Christ;

3. by the demand for inculturation, which produces a variety of contextual christologies particularly suited to the cultural conditions of the different regions of the Church;

4. by an orientation to existential-practical demands, which orientation tends to harmonize orthodoxy and orthopraxy.

This originates multiple visions of christology that form a real theological and pastoral wealth. "Cosmic" christology, for example, presents Jesus as the goal in which the whole universe converges and which sustains, guides, purifies, draws, and brings to fulfillment the evolutionary movement of the cosmos and of all of humanity. "Historical" christology underlines history as the locus of revelation and of the saving application of the mystery of Christ. "Liberation" christology sees in the saving actions of Jesus toward the poor and the marginalized the center of the Christian message and the supreme realization of the kingdom of God. The christology of "popular piety" tries to rediscover the deep theological and pastoral significance of Christian piety. Christology "in context," starting from the historical and cultural originality of a given region of the Church, attempts to elaborate an "inculturated" interpretation of the mystery of Christ.

We will pause briefly to consider a few visions of christology that are particularly suggestive for a renewal of evangelization and catechesis in preparation for the Great Jubilee of the year 2000.

The Mystery of Christ in Catholic "Popular Piety"

Popular Piety: A Basic Reality of Catechesis

"Popular piety" or "popular religiosity" is the true environment of the Church's catechesis and pastoral ministry. The majority of the faithful, whether children or adults, uneducated or cultured, poor or rich, are fully immersed in this climate of popular devotion. They receive, understand, and express the faith, not in the categories of "academic theology," but in particular and specific codes of expression, whose content is often rich in symbols and living experiences. Consequently, popular piety cannot be ignored as irrelevant, or simply superstitious. We must make a place for it as a religious and Christian value.

As early as 1975, Paul VI invited Christians to rediscover popular piety:

> Both in regions where the Church was implanted centuries ago and in those where she is now being implanted, we find among the people distinctive expressions of the search for God and of faith. For a long time these expressions were considered less pure, and were sometimes scorned. However, today they are being rediscovered more or less everywhere. (*EN,* 48)

John Paul II has also exhorted us to make the most of the positive elements in popular piety in catechesis (see *CT,* 54).

Popular Piety Is a "Christian Humanism"

In 1979, the Third General Conference of the Latin American Episcopate, assembled in Puebla, Mexico, described popular piety in its ample and well-known final document:

> By religion of the people, popular piety or religiosity, we mean the ensemble of the deep beliefs sealed by God, the basic attitudes that derive from these convictions, and the expressions that manifest them. We mean the cultural or existential form that religion takes on in a particular people. The religion of the Latin American people, in its most characteristic cultural form, is an expression of the Catholic faith. It is a popular Catholicism." (Puebla, 444)

Popular piety is rich in values that respond with Christian wisdom to the great questions of existence. In fact, this piety has the sense of the sacred, it manifests a thirst for God, and it expresses a moving fervor and purity of intention such as only the simple and the poor can have (see *EN,* 48; *CT,* 54). It is ready to accept the Word of God, it lives the presence of the Trinity (as we see in its devotions and iconography), it believes in Providence and in the loving, faithful presence of God the Father, and it has a great sense of prayer (see *EN,* 48; Puebla, 454, 913). It has a capacity for vital synthesis that creatively unites the divine and the human, Christ and Mary, body and spirit, communion and institution, person and community, faith and country, intelligence and affectivity (see Puebla, 448, 913).

Popular piety is imbued with the awareness of sin and the necessity of expiation (Puebla, 454); it celebrates Christ in the mystery of his Incarnation (Christmas, the Child Jesus), in his crucifixion, in the Eucharist, and in devotion to his Sacred Heart (see Puebla, 454, 912); it enables progress in the knowledge of the mystery of Christ, of his message, of his Incarnation, of his redeeming cross, of his resurrection, of the action of the Spirit in every Christian, and of the mystery of the afterlife (*CT,* 54). It expresses love for Mary, whom it venerates as the immaculate Mother of God and of men, and it enables generosity and sacrifice to the point of heroism when it becomes necessary to defend the faith. It manifests faith in total language (song, images, gestures, color, dance). It overcomes cold rationalisms by setting faith in the context of times (feasts) and in places (shrines and temples). It lives faith with deep intensity by participating in the sacraments of the Church, above all those of reconciliation and the Eucharist.

Popular piety gives rise to inward attitudes rarely seen elsewhere in the same degree: patience, the sense of the cross in daily life, detachment, openness to others, devotion (*EN,* 48), practice of the evangelical virtues (*CT,* 54), detachment from material things, solidarity (Puebla, 454, 913). It has a filial respect for the Church and a true and sincere affection for the person of the Holy Father, whom it enthusiastically perceives to be the teacher and witness of Jesus' goodness in the world (Puebla, 454).

This deep human and Christian wisdom makes popular piety an authentic "Christian humanism that affirms the radical dignity of every person as son of God, establishes a basic brotherhood, teaches us to encounter nature and to understand work, and gives reasons for a certain good humor and wit, even in the midst of a very hard life" (Puebla, 448).

The Need for a "Reeducation" of Popular Piety

We cannot fail to mention the limits and dangers of popular piety, especially when it is ignored and neglected by evangelization and catechesis. The limits of an ancestral type are superstition, magic, fatalism, idolatry of power, fetishism, and ritualism (*EN,* 48; Puebla, 456).

The limits caused by the deformation of catechesis are the following: static archaism, misinformation and ignorance, syncretistic reinterpretation, reduction of faith to a pure contract in one's relation to God, exaggerated regard for the cult of the saints to the detriment of the awareness of Jesus Christ and his mystery (*EN,* 48; Puebla, 456, 914).

The menaces to popular piety also come from secularism, which is spread by the mass media, by consumerism, by the sects, by ideological, economic, and social manipulation, by secularizing political messianisms, by uprooting, and by urban proletarianization due to internal and foreign migrations (Puebla, 456).

Hence the urgency of purification, of ongoing rectification (*CT,* 54), but above all of a continual process of education of popular piety (Puebla, 457, 458–69).

The Figure of Jesus in Popular Piety

The mystery of Jesus Christ is a central element in popular piety. The popular Christ — at whatever level he is understood or "distorted" theologically — is a Christ who is lived, heard, welcomed, loved, and followed by the Christian people. However disfigured and poor may be the reasons for this devotion — often to the advantage of the Blessed Virgin and the saints — this Christ nonetheless illumines and sustains the existence of the people as a whole, becoming the bearer and the guarantor of its noblest values and of its oldest aspirations. Proof of this are participation in the sacraments, especially in the Eucharist; the celebration of the great liturgical feasts devoted to Christ; the practice of devotions to Christ, for example, devotion to the Sacred Heart; his presence as protector of homes through images, altars, and statues.

In the following, we limit ourselves to Latin America and to those countries that have been deeply influenced by centuries of Spanish and Portuguese presence, although what we say could be applied to the popular piety of Italian, Polish, or German influence in North and South America and Australia. Students of folklore and popular piety have identified certain characteristic "images" of Christ in these regions. Particularly vibrant in these nations is devotion to the "dead Christ," with whom the people identifies itself: the famous crucifix of the Church of San Francisco a Bahía in Brazil could be taken as a summary of popular christology in Latin America. There is also a great veneration for the "Baby Jesus," who awakens tenderness; for "Christ the King," who stimulates strength and courage in the difficulties of life and in the persecution of the faith; for "Christ the King of Peace," who was preached by the first evangelizers.

This popular christology calls for a catechesis aimed at a reevangelization that announces without reduction or preconceptions the biblical-ecclesial figure of Christ, true God and true man: "It is our duty to proclaim clearly, leaving no room for doubts or ambiguities, the mystery of the Incarnation: both the divinity of Christ as the Church professes it and the reality and power of his human and historical dimension" (Puebla, 175); "We cannot deform, reduce, or ideologize the person of Christ, whether by making of him a politician, a leader, a revolutionary, or a mere prophet, or by reducing to the merely private sphere him who is the Lord of history" (Puebla, 178; see also 179).

It is thus on the basis of the integral mystery of Christ that the christology of popular piety can give renewed hope to the people, which is often oppressed and humiliated: "In solidarity with the sufferings and the aspirations of our people, we feel the urgent need to give it what is specifically ours to give: the mystery of Jesus of Nazareth, the Son of God. We feel that this is the 'power of God' (Rom 1:16) capable of transforming our personal and social reality and of putting it on the path to freedom and brotherhood, to the full manifestation of the Kingdom of God" (Puebla, 181).

Bringing to fulfillment the christological patrimony of popular religiosity, the Santo Domingo document (1992) focuses the new evangelization of Latin America on the mystery of Christ. It presents Jesus as the "Gospel of the Father," as the "evangelizer living in his Church," and as the "life and hope of Latin America":

Lord Jesus Christ, Son of the living God,
good shepherd and our brother,
our sole option is for you.
United in love and in hope
under the protection of Our Lady of Guadalupe,
star of evangelization,
we invoke your Spirit.
Give us the grace,
in continuity with Medellín and Puebla,
to devote ourselves to a new evangelization,
to which all of us are called,
with a special participation by the laity,
especially the young.
Let us commit ourselves to an ongoing education of faith,
celebrating your praise,
and proclaiming you beyond our borders,
in a decidedly missionary Church....
Give us energies to commit ourselves
to an integral promotion
of the people of Latin America and the Caribbean,
starting from an evangelical and renewed preferential option
for the poor and in service of life and the family.
Help us to work for an inculturated evangelization
that penetrates into the milieux of our cities,
and is incarnated in the indigenous and Afro-American
cultures
through an efficacious educational effort and modern
communication.
Amen. (Santo Domingo, 303)

The "Inculturated" Christ

Inculturation, the Law of All Christian Evangelization
(see GS, 44)

For Vatican II, the history of Christian evangelization has been
and must continue to be a never-ending process of "cultural

adaptation," of "dialogue with cultures," of "vibrant exchange with the various cultures of the peoples" (*GS*, 44, 58). The Church, capitalizing on the treasures hidden in the various forms of human culture,

> learned from the very beginnings of her history to express the mystery of Christ with the help of the concepts and languages of the different peoples; furthermore, she endeavored to explain it with the wisdom of the philosophers: that is, with the aim of adapting, as far as was suitable, the Gospel, whether to the capacity of all or to the demands of the wise. And this adaptation of the preaching of the revealed word has to remain the law of every evangelization. (*GS*, 44)

In this way, the Church appeals to every people's capacity to express the message of Christ according to its particular genius, while at the same time promoting a vibrant exchange within itself. In *Catechesi Tradendae*, John Paul affirms:

> We can say of catechesis, as we do of evangelization in general, that it is called to bring the power of the Gospel into the heart of culture and of cultures. For this reason, catechesis is obliged to try to understand these cultures and their essential elements; to learn their most important expressions; to respect their particular values and treasures. This is the way in which catechesis will succeed in proposing to these cultures the knowledge of the hidden mystery and in helping them to give birth, out of their own living tradition, to original expressions of life, celebration, and thought that are Christian." (53)

Theological and pastoral criteria have recently been worked out in order to foster an authentic inculturation of the Gospel of Christ. A first such criterion is *christological*. In this sense, the process of inculturation is a genuine incarnation of the good news of Jesus in a particular culture, which implies both an appreciation of the good points of that culture and a critique of its human and religious limits.

A second criterion is *ecclesiological.* It sees the Church, both universal and local, as the historical locus and guarantor of the proper outcome of the inculturation process. Thus, it is in the concreteness of ecclesial experience that inculturation is welcomed, lived, discerned, evaluated, and purified — in a word, carried out and fulfilled. Consequently, the Church becomes the historical locus of experience and the criterion of validity and legitimation of every inculturation.

The third criterion is *anthropological.* It underscores the goal of inculturation, which must serve the promotion, illumination, and comprehensive liberation of humankind from the webs of sin, death, injustice, violence, falsehood, and poverty. The inculturation of the faith is an experience of salvation lived by a Christian community in a particular place and in a particular time as the first-fruits of the definitive salvation.

The fourth criterion, that of *dialogue,* ensures that the process of inculturation does not lead to the ghetto of isolation, incapacity to communicate, and opposition to the broader culture, but contributes instead to a greater understanding of the mystery of Christ in the exciting discovery of ever new aspects, which complement and enrich what went before. For this reason, Christian inculturation does not mean marginalization, but interaction, sharing, participation, healthy plurality, and continuous openness to the future. The Holy Spirit brings to maturity the fruits of each culture for the good of all the other Churches and of the universal Church. Cultures do not flourish and develop like separate blades of grass, but like the branches of a single tree.

Christ "in the Cultures"

Acute sensitivity to the originality and unique identity of the various cultural regions of the Church is opening an extremely wide panorama of contextual christologies. Given that we cannot provide a complete map of the various initiatives of inculturation in the Catholic world, we allude only to a few results of this busy workshop of lively activity.

In the Philippines, for example, there are proposals to bring forward and valorize the Christ of Philippine popular piety:

the "Santo Niño," the "Santo Entierro" (holy burial). Further-more, there are endeavors to translate the salvation brought by Christ into categories corresponding to the human and re-ligious experience of the region. For example, the experience of salvation and liberation in Christ is translated with the term "ginhawa" (meaning more or less "well-being"), which derives from the overcoming of "hirap" (all that can block human happiness, from every point of view, including the spiritual). Philippine titles of Jesus can be, for example, *Datung Maraya* (which in Visaya means "he who gives prosperity," and which can be represented by means of the *malunggay* tree, one of the most popular and beneficent plants of the Philippines) or *Ngir Omekuul* (which in Palau means "anchor" and "harbor"), or *Abay* (which in Cebuan means "traveling companion") or *Manluluwas-Kauban* (which on the island of Mindanao indi-cates "he who cares, who gives aid to the hungry, who travels with his people, who protects the persecuted, who pardons sinners, in a word, the liberator").

In India, too, there is a great ferment of inculturation. There are proposals of christologies based on the *guruship* of Jesus (Jesus as teacher of an illuminated and saved life). Jesus is also called *Vimochakan* ("liberator") who practices *ahimsa* (non-violence), and whose arms are love, compassion, hospitality, and committed struggle for the freedom of the oppressed, the victims of discrimination, and the outcasts.

Other proposals come from Bangladesh (Jesus *Uttam Neta:* "good leader"), from Papua New Guinea (Jesus *Kamungo:* "big man," a title already used in the liturgy), from Korea (Jesus *Minjung Mudang:* "healer of the people, for the people, with the people"), from China (Jesus, star that saves), from Taiwan (Jesus, the true *Fu,* source of all prosperity), from Thai-land (Jesus *Pau,* father), from the Australian aborigines (*Walan,* pelican), from Japan (*Dooshi,* teacher).

Inculturation and the question of Christ as the savior of all people are burning issues in Asia. But when it was asked re-cently in the pages of a certain magazine whether there was room for Christ in Asia, the answer of the ecclesial communi-ties was an enthusiastic Yes. For Jesus' saving mystery responds fully to the desires for interiority, liberation, happiness, concord, and endless life of the Asiatic peoples.

Africa is also offering interesting ideas for an inculturation of christology, for example, the idea that Jesus is *head, ancestor, older son, healer, teacher of initiation.* These are names and concepts that could facilitate a better understanding of the figure of Jesus Christ and of his saving mystery. However, the African authors are aware that the mystery of Jesus Christ cannot be totally assimilated and expressed by indigenous categories without losing its originality. In Christ there has to remain an irreducible and untranslatable otherness.

Nevertheless, christological inculturation is not only a theological and pastoral problem facing certain zones of the Church. It concerns the Church as a whole. It is, of course, not a matter of discovering "new faces of Christ," but of giving humanity today the answer to its need for meaning, happiness, dignity, brotherhood, and peace. That is, it is necessary to link the reality of Jesus transmitted to us by the New Testament with the modern world. The possibility of doing so depends on the proposal of a Christian discipleship that begins with new vitality thanks to the rediscovery of the kingdom of God, of the love of God and neighbor, of conversion, of salvation, of mission, of the need for pardon and reconciliation, of the following of Christ, of the Church.

Jesus Christ for Young People

Beyond the geographical inculturation that we have just described, there is also the great "continent" of the young, who have their own distinctive vision of Jesus. The face of Christ that most attracts the young is that of "Christ the Life," whereby Jesus becomes their friend, confidante, brother, the one who pardons them, conquers evil, and is the way and the truth. For young people around the world, Jesus Christ is synonymous with the fullness of humanity, change of life, and liberation. Above all in youthful converts one notices the sense of the liberating presence of Jesus: liberation not only from sin and radical evil, but also from the fears of ancestral piety. One sees too an openness to a new, more joyful life, a freer and more freeing life. Jesus is still today a concrete and meaningful person who has taught us to love, giving an example and paying with his own life. Jesus still excites today's young people who thirst for love, justice, and peace.

A recapitulation of how the young understand Jesus might include the following elements:

1. Jesus is a man engaged in a just "cause" that unites all the energies of his person;

2. this cause is the proclamation of the "kingdom of God" as the gift of happiness and liberation for all, especially for the marginalized, the sick, the oppressed, the weak, women, the excluded, the little ones, the foreigners, the poor;

3. the origin of this earthly and eternal liberation is God, whom Jesus proclaims as the Father, the Son, and the Holy Spirit;

4. the earthly life of Jesus was consistent and harmonious: his deeds corresponded to his words, and this consistency led to his death on the cross;

5. the event of the resurrection was a victorious end, and not a defeat; it brought life, and not death.

This youth christology fills the life of the young with meaning, giving them unity and prospects for personal and communal engagement.

The Challenge of the Christian Model

This synthetic panorama of christologies shows how extraordinarily various and rich the figure of Jesus is in Christians' awareness of faith. We have presented a suggestive palette, which seems to translate — albeit not exhaustively — Saint Paul's wish for the Christians of Ephesus: "that Christ may dwell in your hearts through faith; that you, being rooted and grounded in love, may have power to comprehend with all the saints what is the breadth and length and height and depth, and to know the love of Christ which surpasses knowledge, that you may be filled with all the fulness of God" (Eph 3:17–18).

Let us sum up a few affirmations:

1. Christ is confessed as the savior of man and the way to his complete divinization;

2. the cross is the fulfillment of the mystery of the redemption of man's pain and death;

3. Christ's humanity is seen as the model and source of every authentic humanism;

4. his divine person is seen as the end and fulfillment of the evolutionary process of the cosmos and humanity;

5. his earthly history is seen as the privileged place of dialogue where salvation is offered;

6. his event is seen as the realization of the interior aspiration of man, the "hearer of the word" who is "saved historically by the incarnate Word of God";

7. his message is the authentic liberation from all slavery, poverty, injustice;

8. his presence as the risen Lord is a provident and continuous closeness that greatly inspires the wisdom and the life of the simple and humble folk, which is firmly anchored in the shared and festive celebration of his mysteries of salvation;

9. his event is an impulse for the transformation and renewal of the cultures of the peoples;

10. his mystery is the catalyst for the noblest ideals of the young, who consider him the only and true giver of joy, freedom, and life.

To be sure, even these Christian images are not without their dark sides, such as ignorance, negligent catechesis, tiredness of millennial traditions, the syncretist temptation, undue reductionisms, unilateral emphases, and relativistic impulses. Both the good points and the limits of this summary map of christology are, however, an occasion for christological "reevangelization."

To all this we must add the so-called "christology of the saints," by which is meant the vibrant interpretation of Jesus that the saints have given in their exemplary personal existence. Example are: the poor and joyous Christ of Francis of Assisi, Christ the king and master of Ignatius of Loyola, Christ the Good Samaritan of John of God, Christ the educator of John Bosco. The knowledge and experience that Christians have of Jesus Christ constitute a precious heritage that we must transmit and continue to make fruitful. In fact, it is an inheritance that offers insights that constitute an always valid source for the revitalization of Christian experience today.

Orientations for a New Evangelization of Jesus Today

At this point, however, a number of questions suggest themselves. How do we find our way in this luxurious gallery of portraits of Christ, all of which are equally attractive? Must we use them all, or should we privilege one in particular? And what criteria do we possess for determining the legitimacy of these and other portraits of Jesus?

In short, we ask ourselves: What are the essential points that serve as pillars sustaining the valid images of Jesus Christ? What are the central nuclei of a correct contemporary proclamation of the mystery of Jesus? And how do we live and make live his mystery of salvation in various cultural, social, and categorial contexts?

At this point, let us recall that the specific goal of this theological and pastoral "reflection" (see *TMA*, 40) on Jesus Christ is to develop, promote, and nourish the understanding and the experience of the mystery of Jesus Christ.

It is worth citing the words of John Paul II in *Catechesi Tradendae*:

The aim of catechesis, in the general context of evangelization, is to be the phase of teaching and maturation, that is, the time in which the Christian, having accepted by faith the person of Jesus Christ as the only Lord and having given a total adhesion by a sincere conversion of heart, endeavors to know better this Jesus to whom he has abandoned himself: to know his "mystery," the kingdom of God, which he announces, the demands and the promises contained in his Gospel message, the ways that he has traced for whoever wants to follow him. (*CT,* 20)

In order to respond to the need for a systematic and integral pastoral reproposal of the mystery of Christ, let us make a twofold option.

First of all, let us choose, among the many faces of Jesus, that presented by the *Bible and the Church.* This is the face of Jesus that the Church commits to us in Scripture and in her concrete life of faith. The people of God's bimillennial experience of holiness, of apostolate, of witness, and of salvation is based on the acknowledgment of Christ as the incarnate Son of God, who died and rose for our salvation, and who is the only savior (see Acts 4:12) and "Lord of all" (Acts 10:36). This is the Christ whom the ecclesial community must announce anew, inculturate, and, above all, live — today as yesterday and tomorrow.

The second option concerns the proposal of criteria, not merely criteria pertaining to truth, but existential criteria. In this way, the truth of Jesus Christ becomes life in him and through him.

For this reason we propose three criteria which can serve as a sure platform for an integral proclamation of Jesus Christ — integral both in terms of content and in terms of existential participation:

1. the recounting of the history of Jesus (chapters 4–7);

2. the proclamation of Jesus as the one who lives today in the Church and in the world and as the sole and definitive Savior of humanity (chapter 8);

3. the saving relevance of the mystery of Christ today (chapter 9).

The justification and illustration of these criteria will be the object of the following chapters.

Chapter 4

Telling the Story of Jesus

Jesus and History

Jesus Christ is not a myth. He is not an atemporal idea or ahistorical creation of the first Christian community. Jesus is a historical personage in the full sense of the term. The primary core of every proclamation of Christ is the narration of the story of Jesus, which is the principal source of Christian experience in all times and places. For the story of Jesus of Nazareth — his actions, his words, his attitudes, his teaching, his witness, his death on the cross, his resurrection — *is* the definitive salvation that God offers to every human person. His story is thus a "history of salvation" for every human being and for the whole cosmos.

History is understood here in its full sense. First of all, it is the environment within which some fact has really occurred in a certain time, space, and sociopolitical context. In the second place, it is the locus of revelation, where God's saving plan is realized.

In the first meaning, Jesus is a historical personage who lived at the beginning of the first century of the Christian era (7–4 B.C.–30 A.D.), an era which takes both its name and its beginning from Jesus himself. On this level, Jesus can and should be approached "historically" — as atheists and non-Christians do, for example — insofar as he offers a paradigm of humanity and religion. In consequence, catechesis should not neglect the historical-critical vindication of Jesus Christ and of the Christian sources, not only for the sake of responding to the problem of skepticism — which can go so far as to deny the very historical existence of Jesus — but above all in order to demonstrate the exact correspondence between the historical evidence of the sources and their preeminent purpose of faith.

In the second acceptation, the concrete historical event of Jesus is in itself the revelation and the accomplishment of the mystery of salvation that is the gift of the triune God: "For God so loved the world that he gave his only Son, that whoever believes in him should not perish but have eternal life" (Jn 3:16). This is the theological and salvific side of Jesus' history, which brings salvation to the whole of humankind.

The essential content of our profession of faith is tied to the proclamation of the history of Jesus, the Son of God, who was born, died, and rose again for our salvation. The history of Jesus is the content and the norm of our proclamation of faith, just as it was for the first Christian community.

Peter's preaching is the recounting of the history of Jesus:

> Men of Israel, hear these words: Jesus of Nazareth, a man attested to you by God with mighty works and wonders and signs which God did through him in your midst, as you yourselves know — this Jesus, delivered up according to the definite plan and foreknowledge of God, you crucified and killed by the hands of lawless men. But God raised him up." (Acts 2:22–24)

Every interpretation of Jesus must thus be measured against his history, which is its guarantee and foundation. History is understood here as a complex reality comprising numerous strictly interrelated dimensions. In particular, the event of Christ makes history supremely relevant to salvation. In him, *history* — his word, his actions, the events of his life — is simultaneously *salvation*. The curve of his existence reaches its apex in the paschal mystery of death and resurrection, which are the events of salvation par excellence. The Christ of the Bible is thus the original pole of every christological proclamation.

The Historical Reliability and Biographical Nature of the Gospels

Is it possible to recount the "history" of Jesus? Are the sources historically reliable? Moreover, do they provide material that can be used to tell, for example, the "life" of Jesus? This is a good place to sum up some important findings of contemporary historiography. This will help cut back on the methodical doubt and systematic skepticism concerning the possibility of gaining trustworthy information about who Jesus was and what he did from the Christian sources. In this way, we will clear away some dead weight that still burdens ordinary catechesis.

In the words of John Paul II, "the great event that non-Christian historians do no more than mention is fully illuminated in the writings of the New Testament, which, although they are records of faith, are not less reliable, when their statements are taken as a whole, even as historical evidence" (*TMA, 5*).

The study of the trustworthiness of the Christian sources is at the heart of a heated debate that began in the eighteenth century and has not yet entirely died down. This study is of great importance both for history and for theology. Contemporary research not only tends to be more confident about the historical foundation of the Gospel narratives, but it increasingly sees a very close relation between the Gospels and Greco-Roman biographies of the time. This may be the reason why several lives of Jesus have been published in recent years. We can thus consider that the wheel of hermeneutics has come full circle. After having naively regarded the Gospels as biographies of Jesus, scholarship passed to the clear-cut denial of this appellation, only to return to a critically documented affirmation of their value not only as history, but also as "biography" in the sense of the Hellenistic biographies of the time. It may be useful to give a concise account of this epoch-making turning-point.

The Gospels and Ancient Biography

Clyde Weber Votaw, in an article written in 1915, had assigned the Gospels to the "popular" biographical literature of Greece and Rome, thus putting them on a level with the lives of the philosopher Socrates (469–399 B.C.), the subject of biographies by his disciples Plato (*Dialogues*) and Xenophon (*Memorabilia*); of the wonderworker Apollonius of Tyana (10–97 A.D.), a contemporary of Jesus who found a biographer in Philostratus; of the philosopher Epictetus (50–130 A.D.), whose biography was penned by his disciple Arrian of Nicomedia. Exponents of the method of *Formgeschichte* opposed this biographical interpretation. They regarded the Gospels as mere popular tales and cultic legends having no historical basis or particular biographical purpose.

Students of literary criticism, especially from North America and England (Peter Georgi, David Laurence Barr, Judith L. Wentling, Gilbert G. Bilezikian) have gradually overcome the prejudice that treats the Gospels as so many legendary tales. An important contribution to this reevaluation of the historical and biographical reliability of the Gospels has been made by Graham N. Stanton, whose studies have shown, among other things, that Luke's Gospel is a mine of information on the life and the character of Jesus of Nazareth. In his examination of ancient biographies, Stanton observes, furthermore, that many of these lack elements considered important today, such as chronology and the development of the psychological character of the protagonist. He concludes that the Gospels are biographical writings, even though they have characteristics that set them apart from their modern counterparts.

In 1978, Charles Talbert likewise placed all the Gospels in the genre of biography; in 1982, Philip Shuler established the biographical character of Matthew's Gospel. In the work published by Hubert Cancik in 1984, it was demonstrated that the genre of Mark was the *bíos* (life). In the same year, Klaus Berger published in the prestigious *Aufstieg und Niedergang der Römischen Welt* a study entitled "Hellenistic Genres in the New Testament." In this very thorough monograph, Berger insists that the Gospels are extremely close to the *bíoi* (lives) of the ancient philosophers. Completing almost a century of studies in this line, Richard A. Burridge could affirm in 1992 that the growing tendency among New Testament scholars to regard the Gospels as "biographies" is well-founded; that it is therefore high time to apply the adjective "biographical" to the Gospels, inasmuch as they are nothing less than lives of Jesus.

Comparing the Gospels to the biographical literature of the Greco-Roman and Hebrew worlds, we find convincing reasons for believing the Gospels to be lives of Jesus. Concretely,

Burridge analyzes the following ten lives: (1) the *Evagoras* of
Isocrates (436–338 B.C.), a prose encomium in honor of the
king of Cyprus; (2) the *Agesilaos* of Xenophon (428–354 B.C.),
likewise an encomium in honor of the king of Sparta, which
contains a great deal of historical material; (3) the *Euripides*
of Satiros, an author of lives in the peripatetic tradition (third
century B.C.?); (4) the *Atticus* of Cornelius Nepos (first century
B.C.), which is part of *De viris illustribus,* the first example of
Roman biography; (5) the *Moses* of Philo of Alexandria (30/25
B.C.–45 A.D.), the biography of a biblical personage; (6) Tacitus's *Agricola,* written in 95 A.D. to honor the consul Julius
Agricola; (7) *Cato Minor* by Plutarch (45–120 A.D.), one of
the *Parallel Lives;* (8) *The Lives of the Caesars* of Gaius Sue-
tonius Tranquillus (born in 69 A.D., date of death unknown);
(9) the *Demonax* of Lucian (120–80 A.D.); (10) the *Apollonius
of Tyana* of Philostratus (170–250 A.D.).

The chief characteristic of this genre is its exclusive attention
to the subject. All of these works concentrate on the person
who is the only protagonist of the writing. However, the tradition is very supple; sometimes a work will cover the entire
life of the hero, sometimes only one period of it; sometimes
it concentrates on the facts and on chronology, sometimes on
certain themes, teachings, or virtues, without proceeding in
chronological order.

The Biographical Character of the Gospels

Burridge applies to the synoptics and to John the same analysis
used in dealing with the ten biographies that we have just men-
tioned. We limit ourselves here to a few conclusions that are
useful for our subject.

Concerning the *introductory notes,* Burridge emphasizes, for
example, that Matthew begins with the genealogy of Jesus,
a characteristic element of the *bíos* genre. Similarly, the prologue of Luke's Gospel (1:1–4) is an actual historiographical
introduction similar to the prologues of the Greco-Roman
biographical literature of the time.

In the second place, the *subject* of the Gospels is Jesus alone.
Jesus is the key personage who takes center stage: the other

characters revolve around him. The spotlight is always on Jesus. In this sense, the Gospels differ from the Acts of the Apostles, where the protagonists of the narrative are the Apostles, above all Peter and Paul. An analysis of the subjects of the verbs confirms the observation that the Gospels focus exclusively on Jesus: Jesus is the subject of approximately a fourth of the verbs (24.4 percent). Another fifth refer to his words, his teaching, and his parables (20.2 percent). No other character receives more than 1 percent of the attention. The disciples singly and collectively get 12.2 percent; those to whom Jesus speaks and whom he helps 9.3 percent; all the rest get 5 percent.

Moreover, the Gospels concentrate on the last three years of Jesus' life, especially his death. This absence of references to the earlier years has often been presented as a weighty objection against regarding the Gospels as biographies. In reality, in the ten ancient biographies that Burridge examines, the first thirty or forty years of the heroes' lives are either treated very briefly or even omitted; the accent is placed on the decisive period of their life and death.

The statistical analysis of the amount of space set aside for the passion and death of Jesus leads to the following conclusions. Matthew and Luke devote 15 percent of their narrative to Jesus' Last Supper, passion, death, and resurrection; Mark dedicates 19.1 percent of his Gospel to these events. If we compare this with the amount of space that the ancient Greek and Roman lives devote to the last acts of their heroes, we find that this is normal: in Plutarch the percentage is 17.3, in Nepos 15, in Tacitus 10, in Philostratus 26. The Evangelists' concentration on Jesus' passion and death is thus no argument against the biographical character of the Gospels. This allows us to go beyond the commonplace originated by Martin Kähler, who observed that Mark is the story of the passion with an ample introduction. The truth is, as we have already said, that the passion takes up only 19 percent of the narrative, nor can we regard the remaining 80.1 percent as a mere introduction. Moreover, the analysis of the development of the three synoptics shows that the Evangelists are narrating a story with a precise geographical progression, the final goal of which is Jerusalem, and a chronological structure that extends from Jesus' birth or public ministry to his passion and death. Each Evangelist places his thematic material in this spatio-temporal framework.

Regarding the *mode of characterization,* some assert that the Gospels lack any physical and psychological presentation of Jesus. However, this is a requirement above all of modern biographies. In general, the ancient method inferred the character of the person from his sayings and deeds. Luke says it plainly: unlike Acts, his Gospel treats of what Jesus began to do and to teach (see Acts 1:1). Instead of speaking abstractly of charity and acceptance, the Gospels portray Jesus as available and understanding toward the needy. We have, in other words, an indirect characterization, which is no less effective and complete for being so. Like the biographers, the Evangelists tend to sketch their subject not by offering a photograph of Jesus, but a portrait, that is, a picture that presupposes interpretation and meditation. We do not have abstract and stereotypical, but concrete and original characterizations.

Everything that is said about the synoptics can be said of the Gospel of John, who is generally thought to be less interested in what Jesus did than in making theological statements. In reality, manual analysis of the subjects of the verbs in the Fourth Gospel shows that more than a fifth (20.2 percent) have Jesus as their subject. If we add the subjects of the sayings referred to Jesus we get 55.3 percent, a sum even higher than in the synoptics. The conclusion is rather surprising: John is interested in the activity of Jesus both in narration and in teaching. Moreover, a third of the Gospel is dedicated to Jesus' final week, his farewell, and his passion and death. This is not foreign to the genre. This becomes evident when we compare John with, for example, the *Agesilaos* of Xenophon, in which 37 percent of the narrative deals with the Persian campaign, and with Philostratus's *Apollonius of Tyana,* in which 26.3 percent of the narrative is taken up with the dialogues of the imprisonment, the trial, and the death.

In conclusion, we have good reason to call the Gospels "biographical," inasmuch as they can be regarded as genuine lives of Jesus — in conformity with the literary conception of the time, to be sure. Consequently, the Gospels are not only the history of the Christian experience of the first ecclesial communities. This can be said of the Letters of Saint Paul, of the Acts of the Apostles, of Revelation. The Gospels, on the other hand, are focused on Jesus, on his words, his attitudes, his deeds of power, and, above all, on the saving event of his death and resurrection. The first Christian community would not have produced the Gospels as "lives" if it had not been interested in the historical person of Jesus, the source and foundation of its own existence of faith, prayer, mission, service, and testimony.

Evangelization: Telling the Story of Jesus

Following the example of the primitive Christian community, we must once again integrally proclaim in our day the words and actions of Jesus of Nazareth. We have to take up the Gospels again and reread the Word of God as light, spirit, and life.

Narration was, in fact, the principal expression of primitive Christian catechesis (see Lk 1:1–4). The discourses of Peter and Paul contained in the Acts of the Apostles are nothing but a telling of the story of Jesus. The four Gospels can be seen as four manuals for living faith in Christ. If the story of Jesus recounted by Mark can prepare catechumens for conversion, the story told by Matthew offers the newly baptized the best way to live the following of Christ. The Gospel of Luke and the Acts of the Apostles aid all the faithful in taking up a life of evangelical and missionary witness. Finally, mature Christians will find in the story of Jesus as told by John an authentic handbook of christocentric and trinitarian spirituality.

Narration has to be seen not so much as information, but as an authentic and complex work of communicating the faith, of representing the saving events, of existential probing, of conversion, of invitation to a coherent apostolate.

The most fitting tool for an edifying, interiorized reading of the history of Jesus by persons and communities is the *lectio divina,* that is, a prayerful reading of the Gospels. In this *lectio,* Jesus' word is not only listened to and meditated upon, but above all prayed and inwardly accepted. Kept in the heart of the faithful, it brings them to a continuous conversion and a harmonious apostolic witness.

As elements of meditation, we propose here in synthesis the most important aspects of the story of Jesus: his preaching, the paschal mystery of death and resurrection, his birth.

Chapter 5

Jesus Announces the Good News

Jesus' Pedagogy

The "good news" of the kingdom that Jesus preached and practiced was his victory over physical, psychic, and spiritual evil. When John had sent his disciples to find out who he was, Jesus answered: "Go and tell John what you hear and see: the blind receive their sight and the lame walk, lepers are cleansed and the deaf hear, and the dead are raised up, and the poor have the good news preached to them" (Mt 11:4–6).

Jesus' preaching was not an insubstantial *flatus vocis,* but an immediate, healing intervention of God, who gives man life, restoring his health and psychological balance, and liberating him from the power of the evil one. In Jesus there was a perfect harmony and correspondence between action and behavior, between being and action. In his preaching the proclamation of salvation became the immediate experience of physical health, psychological freedom, and spiritual liberation.

Significant in this regard is the episode of the paralytic of Capharnaum, which is told by the three synoptics:

And behold, they brought to him a paralytic, lying on his bed; and when Jesus saw their faith, he said to the paralytic, "Take heart my son; your sins are forgiven." And behold, some of the scribes said to themselves, "This man is blaspheming." But Jesus, knowing their thoughts, said, "Why do you think evil in your hearts? For which is easier to say, 'Your sins are forgiven,' or to say, 'Rise and walk'? But that you may know that the Son of man has authority on earth to forgive sins"— he then said to the paralytic— "Rise, take up your bed, and go home." And he rose and went home. (Mt 9:2–7)

In this episode, physical healing is nothing but the visible face of the spiritual miracle of liberation from sin. Healing and pardoning are the typical gestures of Jesus' pedagogy.

Jesus Welcomes the Poor and the Marginalized

One of the best established facts of the story of Jesus is his closeness to sinners and the marginalized, so much so that he is called a "glutton and a drunkard, a friend of tax collectors and sinners" (Mt 11:19). These are apparently titles of censure and disapproval. In reality, these epithets correspond to how Jesus actually behaved. For him, the nearness of the kingdom was the saving nearness of God to all the marginalized of his time, victims of rejection, segregation, inequality, injustice, sin, and evil.

The list of the poor and needy is always a long one in every epoch and every society. In Jesus' time, there was a vast multitude of people discriminated against and excluded because of illness, income, religion, or immoral behavior. Jesus had limitless compassion for them: "When he saw the crowds, he had compassion for them, because they were harassed and helpless, like sheep without a shepherd" (Mt 9:36). Before the multiplication of the loaves, Jesus "saw a great throng; and he had compassion on them, and healed their sick" (Mt 14:14).

Acceptance, compassion, understanding, and forgiveness were habitual attitudes of Jesus toward that throng of needy people who approached him every day: publicans, sinners, prostitutes, criminals, foreigners, lepers, widows, children, the sick, the suffering, the possessed, renegades, enemies, the poor, even those who crucified him. Jesus had a particular regard for the poor and the despised: "Blessed are the poor in spirit, for theirs is the kingdom of heaven" (Mt 5:3). This poverty of spirit is a lack of outward goods lived with an inward attitude of confidence, gratitude, and absolute faith in divine providence. Even if in relation to the rich, Jesus adopts an understanding attitude (see Mk 10:21), poverty is nevertheless the ideal of the true Christian: "If you would be perfect, go, sell what you possess and give to the poor, and you will have treasure in heaven; and come, follow me" (Mt 19:21).

Jesus Forgives and Converts Sinners

The publicans or tax collectors were hated by the people because they collaborated with the Roman invaders and because they were unjust and exorbitant. It was considered compromising to associate with them. In fact, they were classed with the sinners and the prostitutes (see Mt 9:10; 21:31–32; Mk 2:15; Lk 15:1). The friendly attitude of Jesus, who sat at table with them, was thus unconventional, if not downright scandalous and unseemly: "And as he sat at table in the house, many tax collectors and sinners came and sat down with Jesus and his disciples" (Mt 9:10). Jesus did not abstain from speaking to these notorious social outcasts because he wanted to instruct and convert them. Indeed, he calls the publican Matthew to follow him, making him his disciple (see Mt 9:9), and presents as a model of true prayer, not the presumptuous and proud Pharisee, but the humble publican who declares himself a sinner before God (see Lk 18:10–13).

Significant is Jesus' meeting with Zacchaeus, chief tax collector of Jericho. Desirous of seeing Jesus, Zacchaeus, because of the crowd and his shortness, climbed up a sycamore tree:

> And when Jesus came to the place, he looked up and said to him, "Zacchaeus, make haste and come down; for I must stay at your house today." So he made haste and came down, and he received him joyfully. (Lk 19:5–6)

Jesus' meeting with Zacchaeus exemplifies man's search for the realization of his vocation to happiness. Zacchaeus "was a chief tax collector, and rich," and everyone considered him a "sinner" (see Lk 19:2, 7). Nevertheless, despite his ill-gotten wealth and his great concern to administer and multiply it, Zacchaeus wanted to see Jesus and meet the man who had restored happiness to the blind man on the outskirts of the city (see Lk 18:35–43). His motive is more than mere curiosity; he seems at-

tracted by the irresistible force of the good, by the intense desire
to receive the gift of inner sight in order to change his existence.

Zacchaeus has to choose between remaining in sin and injustice and opening to the call of the good and of righteousness.
Jesus' word directs him once and for all to the choice of the
good: " 'Make haste and come down.' So he made haste and
came down... " (Lk 19:5–6). It is the favorable time of the call
of grace, which demands a ready and convinced response. Zacchaeus perceives that the utopia of happiness is providentially
within reach. It is necessary to make haste to move from an attitude of pure curiosity, of noninvolvement in the good, perhaps
even of pride, to an attitude of conversion and of performance
of the good in the actions of everyday life.

Noteworthy is the saving significance of the simple adverb
"today." It represents the concentrate of the life of every human
person, which is essentially "today," that is, "time" — past,
present, and future. The past is made up of so many "todays"
no longer in our possession. The future will be made up of
many "todays" that we have not yet known and lived through.
And the present is the "today" which we have to reach happiness. And it is in the present, now, that Jesus is calling us to
meet him, awaiting man's willingness to welcome him: "Behold,
I stand at the door and knock; if anyone hears my voice and
opens the door, I will come into him and eat with him, and he
with me" (Rev 3:20).

We can extract from Luke's Gospel an extraordinary theology of the "today" of salvation, in which our destiny of
happiness is at stake. The Evangelist often uses this word in relation to Jesus. At Jesus' birth, the angel says to the shepherds:
"to you is born this day in the city of David a Savior, who is
Christ the Lord" (Lk 2:11). In the synagogue of Nazareth, Jesus
applies to himself the prophecy of Is 61:1ff: "Today this scripture has been fulfilled in your hearing" (Lk 4:21). In the face
of the healing of the paralytic, the crowd exclaims filled with
awe: "We have seen strange things today" (Lk 5:26). To Peter,
who in words was ready to go to prison and die for his master,
Jesus answers: "I tell you, Peter, the cock will not crow this day,
until you three times deny that you know me" (Lk 22:34). And

Peter, remembering that Jesus had told him "before the cock crows today, you will deny me three times,... went out and wept bitterly" (Lk 22:61–62). To the crucified criminal who asked Jesus to remember him, Jesus answers, "Truly, I say to you, today you will be with me in paradise" (Lk 23:43). The "today" is thus the time of salvation in which Jesus is born for us, performs for us his miracles of healing, suffers our repeated denials, and gives eternal salvation: "Today you will be with me in paradise."

Jesus, the risen and "living one" (Rev 1:18) repeats his invitation: "I must stay at your house today." He speaks to humankind searching for happiness and salvation. Zacchaeus understands that the time to change has come. He makes haste and comes down from the tree and joyfully receives Jesus (see Lk 19:6). The Psalmist says, "Let the hearts of those who seek the Lord rejoice" (Ps 105:3). Zacchaeus's joy expresses authentic conversion. For his hospitality means recognition of his sinful situation and immediate willingness to change, an attitude that is revealed not only in words, but in concrete deeds: "Behold, Lord, the half of my goods I give to the poor; and if I have defrauded any one of anything, I restore it fourfold" (Lk 19:8).

Zacchaeus begins a new life, a life of reconciliation, not only with God, but also with the brothers defrauded by his greed. A life of "sharing": "the half of my goods I give to the poor." There is a hint of involuntary irony in Zacchaeus's words, or perhaps of humility and acceptance of his own limitations. Zacchaeus is not yet an absolute saint, as, for example, Saint Francis of Assisi would have been, who distributed not the "half," but "all" of his goods to the poor. Nevertheless, Zacchaeus's restitution of his ill-gotten gains is a true act of conversion to the virtue that he has neglected. It is a recovery of authenticity and happiness.

Virtue, as the practical performance of the good, is, in fact, the principle that gives rise to true happiness: "Desire for true happiness frees man from his immoderate attachment to the goods of this world so that he can find his fulfillment in the vision and beatitude of God" (CCC, 2548). For true happiness is not an already given good, but a good to be created with inventiveness, shrewdness, and wisdom.

Jesus Heals the Sick

Christ the wonderworker and physician of bodies and souls is a title based on the reality of the earthly Jesus. In Jesus' times, of course, the scientific knowledge that we have today about diseases and the microorganisms that can cause them did not exist. Nor was there an adequate theoretical understanding of mental illnesses. Nor was there surgery of any note, at least not in Israel, with the exception of circumcision, which, however, was more socioreligious than properly therapeutic in nature. The rules of hygiene were likewise rudimentary, if not altogether lacking. The same is true of cures and medicines, which were often nothing better than diets (Lk 8:55), ointments and poultices (see Is 1:6; 38:21), eyewashes (Rev 3:18), and baths (Jn 5:4). The New Testament contains descriptions of physical disabilities such as deafness and muteness (see Mk 7:31–37), epilepsy (see Lk 9:38; Mt 17:14), dropsy (Lk 14:2), hemorrhages (see Mt 9:20–22), etc.

Jesus' activity as a healer is one of the first and best attested episodes of the New Testament: "And he went about all Galilee, teaching in their synagogues and preaching the gospel of the kingdom and healing every disease and every infirmity among the people. So his fame spread throughout all Syria, and they brought him all the sick, those afflicted with various diseases and pains, demoniacs, epileptics, and paralytics, and he healed them" (Mt 4:23–24; see Mt 9:35; 14:34–36; 15:30–31).

There are numberless miracles of healing. Jesus heals Peter's mother-in-law of fever with a gesture of great tenderness: "he touched her hand, and the fever left her" (Mt 8:15). He heals the paralytic, whose sins he also forgives (see Mt 9:1–8). He restores health to the woman who for twelve years had suffered a loss of blood (see Mt 9:20–22). He restores sight to the blind (see Mt 9:27–31; 20:29–34; Mk 8:22–26). An extraordinary case is that of the young man born blind whose healing at Jesus' hands fills not only the crowd, but his own parents with amazement (see Jn 9:1–41). He restores hearing and speech to a deaf-mute (Mk 7:31–37) and the use of his joints to a man with a withered hand (see Mt 12:9–14). He heals an epileptic (see Mt 17:14–21), a dropsical man (see Lk 14:1–6), and a stooped woman who had been sick for eighteen years (see Lk 13:10–17).

Once Jesus himself went to a man suffering from a chronic illness who had been totally abandoned for thirty-eight years. Finding himself in Jerusalem, he went to the pool of Bethzatha, with its five porticoes in which lay a multitude of invalids, blind, lame, and paralyzed:

> One man was there, who had been ill for thirty-eight years. When Jesus saw him and knew that he had been lying there a long time, he said to him, "Do you want to be healed?" The sick man answered him, "Sir, I have no man to put me into the pool when the water is troubled, and while I am going another steps down before me." Jesus said to him, "Rise, take up your pallet, and walk." And at once the man was healed, and he took up his pallet and walked. (Jn 5:5–9)

It is likely that this pool was — or had been — a sort of pagan sanctuary dedicated to Asclepios, the Greek god of healing. In the porticoes a large number of "invalids, blind, lame, paralyzed" would gather (Jn 5:3). The pool with its abundance of fresh spring water had power to restore health. Jesus takes the initiative: "Do you want to be healed?" (Jn 5:6).

This paralytic gives us a view of humanity in the extreme marginalization of illness and solitude. Every day the paralytic sees other sick people who are brought to the waters to heal, whereas he remains alone and incapable of moving. He no longer has the courage and strength to cry out like the ten lepers, "Jesus, Master, have pity on us" (Lk 17:13). No one takes notice of him. Big cities and their anonymous crowds often hide silent dramas of marginalization and loneliness. Jesus comes to all people to offer them his water of life in many different ways: with the word of the Gospel, with his eucharistic presence in the community of the Church, with the hospitality, help, and solidarity of good and virtuous men. This is a special antidote to the loneliness and marginalization of poor, sick, old, unemployed, and desperate foreigners.

Jesus conquers not only sin and diseases, but also Satan. Jesus liberates men possessed by the devil: "That evening they brought him many who were possessed with demons; and he cast out the spirits with a word, and healed all who were sick" (Mt 8:16). He healed the two mad demoniacs of Gadara (see Mt 8:28–34; Mk 5:1–20; Lk 8:26–39), the demoniac from Capharnaum (Mk 1:21–28; Lk 4:31–37), a mute demoniac (see Mt 9:32–34), another who is blind and deaf (Mt 12:22–24).

It is true that at that time disturbances, functional disorders, and diseases like epilepsy were regarded as consequences of diabolical possession. However, in his struggle with those possessed by demons, Jesus faces not only sick persons, but the adversary of the good, the tempter and seducer of man. And Jesus conquers him. Jesus' power is greater than Satan. When he performs exorcisms, Jesus is not only healing a disease, but expelling the adversary of God's kingdom. In the struggle between good and evil, Jesus is the victor over Satan.

Jesus Honors Women

Jesus' attitude toward women is a further example of his willingness to receive the oppressed and the marginalized in a way that gives them a new lease on life. Because of this way of acting, he has been considered the model of true humanity. The witness of the Gospel is univocal. Jesus received women, he esteemed them, he respected them, he fully appreciated their potential. He lived in a male-centered society and culture that discriminated against women, who found themselves thwarted and humiliated in their fundamental rights as persons. Women were the property first of their fathers, then of their husbands; they did not have the right to give witness; they could not even learn the Torah.

In this atmosphere of prejudice, Jesus acted without animosity, but with freedom and courage. He approaches women and heals them. He does not discriminate against foreign women (he heals the daughter of the Syro-Phoenecian woman: Mk 7:24–30). He overcomes the taboo concerning their impurity under the law (he heals the woman diseased with an issue of blood: Mk 5:34), holds them up as an example (he lauds the poor widow: Mk 12:41–44), cultivates their friendship (he is a close friend of Martha and Mary, the sisters of Lazarus: Lk 10:38–42; Jn 11).

Strikingly novel is Jesus' attitude of mercy toward those women who were despised as sinners or adulterers, such as the public sinner who enters into the Pharisee's house in order to anoint Jesus' feet with perfumed oil (Lk 7:37–47), or the woman taken in adultery (Jn 8:3–11).

We find an important example of this attitude in Jesus' colloquy with the Samaritan woman. She was a non-Jewish woman and a well-known sinner, inasmuch as she had had five husbands, and the man with whom she was then living was not her husband. This was a particularly serious situation, so much so that the disciples "marveled that he was talking with a woman" (Jn 4:27). Nevertheless, Jesus stops to talk with her, manifests to her the mystery of the Father, of trinitarian adoption, and of his own person:

> Jesus said to her, "Woman, believe me, the hour is coming when neither on this mountain nor in Jerusalem will you worship the Father. You worship what you do not know; we worship what we know, for salvation is from the Jews. But the hour is coming, and now is, when the true worshippers will worship the Father in spirit and truth...."
> The woman said to him, "I know that Messiah is coming (he who is called Christ); when he comes, he will show us all things." Jesus said to her, "I who speak to you am he."
> (Jn 4:21–26)

For Jesus, the woman was as capable as the man of penetrating into the great truths of religion, of accepting them, of living them, and of proclaiming them in turn. In fact, the Samaritan woman becomes a disciple and messenger among the inhabitants of her village: "Many Samaritans from that city believed in him because of the woman's testimony" (Jn 4:39). Not only that, but Martha pronounces, like Peter, an enthusiastic profession of faith: "Yes, Lord; I believe that you are the Christ, the Son of God, he who is coming into the world" (Jn 11:27).

The women with Jesus become adults and overcome the apartheid of their culture. It was they who accompanied Jesus to the cross without betraying him (see Mt 27:55). For their fidelity Jesus gave them the joy of being the first to tell the news of his resurrection. Appearing to Mary Magdalene, Jesus entrusts to her the first joyful message: "Mary Magdalene went and said to the disciples, 'I have seen the Lord'; and she told them that he had said these things to her" (Jn 20:18).

Analyzed in the light of depth psychology, Jesus' behavior gets very positive marks: it is the attitude of a balanced and extraordinarily harmonious man. The source of this attitude is neither the culture of the time, which was markedly male-centered, nor simply opposition to this culture.

In reality, Jesus obeys the law of creation and redemption. His criterion of judgment is what was at the "beginning," when man and woman enjoyed equal dignity and nobility (see Gn 1:27). For those who say that Moses allowed a man to write a certificate of divorce, Jesus confirms that "in the beginning" (see Mk 10:6) it was not so. He knows the reality of creation and is aware that not only the man, but also the woman is the image of God. He also knows that the image of the human person, which is disfigured by sin, is restored by the mystery of his Incarnation. His frame of reference is thus the beginning and the fullness of time. Indeed, in the mystery of Jesus, man and woman recover the splendor of their authentic image as children of God endowed with equal dignity and nobility. In Jesus "there is neither Jew nor Greek, there is neither slave nor free, there is neither male nor female" (Gal 3:28).

Jesus Welcomes the Needy
and Defends the Lowly and the Weak

Thanks to his exemplary attitude, Jesus appears as every man's brother. Having taught and practiced availability to others, Jesus bequeathed this same attitude on Calvary: "He said to his mother, 'Woman, behold your son!' Then he said to the disciple, 'Behold your mother!' And from that hour the disciple took her to his own home" (Jn 19:26–27).

The reward of eternal communion with God will depend on whether we have welcomed Jesus in our needy brothers:

> "Come, O blessed of my Father, inherit the kingdom prepared for you from the foundation of the world; for I was hungry and you gave me food, I was thirsty and you gave me drink, I was a stranger and you welcomed me, I was naked and you clothed me, I was sick and you visited me, I was in prison and you came to me." Then the righteous will answer him, "Lord, when did we see the hungry and feed thee, or thirsty and give thee drink? And when did we see thee a stranger and welcome thee, or naked and clothe thee? And when did we see thee sick or in prison and visit thee?" And the King will answer them, "Truly, I say to you, as you did it to one of the least of these my brethren, you did it to me." (Mt 25:34–40)

As he was "teaching his disciples" (see Mk 9:31), Jesus "took a child, and put him in the midst of them; and taking him in his arms, he said to them, 'Whoever receives one such child in my name receives me; and whoever receives me, receives not me but him who sent me" (vv. 36–37). The disciples had been arguing about who was the greatest in the kingdom of heaven. Jesus answers these men, who were adults and had experienced life, with a symbolic gesture: the greatest is the least, the first is the last, the master is the servant of all, the true adult in the kingdom of heaven is the child. It is not children who have to become like adults, but the adults who must become like the children.

In order to understand the novelty of Jesus' way of acting, we need to take a look at the culture of his time. On the one hand, the Greeks and the Romans abandoned or ruthlessly eliminated sick or maimed children or unwanted baby girls. On the other hand, they idealized children as a symbol of beauty and of the presence of the gods: "Maxima debetur puero reverentia" (the child is owed the highest respect), said Juvenal. The Hebrew tradition likewise had scant regard for children, seeing in them the deficiencies and imperfections of an immature and fragile being.

Jesus' positive attitude was unmistakable: "Let the children come to me, and do not hinder them; for to such belongs the kingdom of heaven" (Mt 19:14). For him it is above all the little ones who understand the things of God: "I thank thee, Father, Lord of heaven and earth, that thou hast hidden these things from the wise and understanding, and revealed them to babes; yea, Father, for such was thy gracious will" (Lk 10:21). For this reason, Jesus invites adults to conversion: "Truly, I say to you, unless you turn and become like children, you will never enter the kingdom of heaven. Whoever humbles himself like this child, he is the greatest in the kingdom of heaven" (Mt 18:3–4). "To such belongs the kingdom of heaven" (Mk 10:13).

The child becomes the image of Jesus: "Whoever receives one such child in my name receives me" (Mt 18:5). Indeed, to receive a child is also to receive the Father: "Whoever receives one such child in my name receives me; and whoever receives me, receives not me but him who sent me" (Mk 9:37). Furthermore, to take care of children by educating, instructing, and receiving them is to be saved: "Come, O blessed of my Father, inherit the kingdom prepared for you from before the foundation of the world; for I was hungry and you gave me food...as you did it to one of the least of these my brethren, you did it to me" (Mt 25:34–35, 40).

In the children it is Jesus himself who asks to be rescued from Herod and his assassins, just as he was defended by Joseph and his mother when they took flight into Egypt (see Mt 2:13–23). The little ones must be received and protected, not humiliated, scandalized, or killed: "Whoever causes one of these little ones who believe in me to sin, it would be better for him to have a great millstone fastened round his neck and to be drowned in the depth of the sea" (Mt 18:6).

Only Luke makes fleeting reference to Jesus' childhood. He recounts the episode of Jesus' being lost in the temple in Jerusalem and makes a general statement to the effect that "the child grew and became strong, filled with wisdom; and the favor of God was upon him" (Lk 2:40). Jesus had first-hand experience of being an "infant." He knew what it was like to be without words, though he was the Word; to be weak, though he was the Mighty One; to be obedient to Mary and Joseph, though he was the Lord of all; to be a fragment of time, though he was eternity. Jesus experienced the maternal tenderness of Mary and the protection of Joseph. He knows that to be a child is to abandon oneself completely to others, to depend on others, to learn from others.

There is a second reason why Jesus valued children so highly. He is the Son of the Father. Even though he grows, he remains forever the "Son," he who is in the bosom of the Father, in the arms of divine charity. This is the major theological reason that impels Jesus to dictate the law of childhood: all of us are and remain children of the Father, protected by the great mercy and charity of the Father. The human family that God has created is a family of sons of God and of brothers in Christ. This is why "whoever does not receive the kingdom of God like a child shall not enter it" (Mk 10:15).

The praise of the little ones does not mean immaturity and imperfection, but confidence and simplicity. Saint Paul admonishes us to be "babes in evil" (1 Cor 14:20). That is, we must not grow in evil, but in goodness. This is why Saint Paul was glad of his infirmities and limits: "For when I am weak, then I am strong" (2 Cor 12:10). "God chose what is foolish in the world to shame the wise, God chose what is weak in the world to shame the strong... so that no human being might boast in the presence of God" (1 Cor 1:27, 29).

Jesus Teaches Forgiveness and Love of Enemies

In order to vanquish the alienation of rancor and revenge, Jesus teaches us to pardon those who offend and persecute us. Unlike the Essenes of Qumran, who admitted only the "pure," Jesus announces that even the lost are invited to the table of the kingdom: "For the Son of man came to seek and save the lost" (Lk 19:9–10). He forgives the Apostle Peter for having denied him (Jn 21:15–19). He pardons the disciples who had abandoned him, and he forgives his very executioners: "Father, forgive them; for they know not what they do" (Lk 23:34).

Jesus educates us to mercy and forgiveness by word and example: "For if you forgive men their trespasses, your heavenly Father will also forgive you" (Mt 6:14); "if your brother... repents, forgive him" (Lk 17:3–4). In the parable of the prodigal Son, Jesus shows how great is the merciful heart of God the Father in pardoning the sins of his ungrateful sons (see Lk 15:11–32).

Jesus himself is the incarnate mercy of God. His gesture of forgiveness is not simply the tolerant attitude of a generous man who, being himself a sinner, is understanding toward the sin of others. Rather, it is a gesture of absolute goodness on the part of one who is innocent and who uproots evil from sinners' hearts, converting them to the good and to charity. In the parable of the lost sheep, Jesus states that "it is not the will of my Father in heaven that one of these little ones should perish" (Mt 18:14). In Luke, Jesus' word is even more radical: "Just so, I tell you, there will be more joy in heaven over one sinner who repents than over ninety-nine righteous persons who need no repentance" (Lk 15:7).

"Then Peter came up and said to him, 'Lord, how often shall my brother sin against me, and I forgive him? As many as seven times?' Jesus said to him, 'I do not say to you seven times, but seventy times seven'" (Mt 18:21–22). And immediately after the parable of the unmerciful debtor, Jesus concludes his teaching saying, "So also my heavenly Father will do to every one of you, if you do not forgive your brother from your heart" (Mt 18:35).

The Christian is called to pardon always. Jesus' merciful example was imitated literally by the first Christian martyr, Saint Stephen, who died pardoning his executioners: "Lord, do not hold this sin against them" (Acts 7:59–60). Ever since then, all Christian martyrs have forgiven their executioners, inaugurating a culture of pardon and peace which still today constitutes the Christian Gospel.

Is forgiveness strength or weakness, victory or defeat, hope or renunciation? Pardon is a gesture of love and courage. Pardon restores to the sinner his dignity as a man, which has been ruined and disfigured by his sin. With pardon the killers will no longer raise their hands to strike an innocent person. Pardon restores to man his dignity as a son of God. Pardon is the virtue of the strong.

Jesus completes the hard lesson of forgiveness with his teaching on love of enemies. It is a doctrine that seems impossible to put into practice, because man's nature demands justice, harmony, and balance. Whoever does good, receives good. Whoever does evil, merits evil. This is justice. Man, when evil has been done to him, sees only two possible attitudes: that of vengeance and that of justice.

Jesus opposes revenge and surpasses human justice with the attitude of pardon and love for one's enemies:

> You have heard that it was said, "An eye for an eye and a tooth for a tooth." But I say to you, Do not resist one who is evil. But if anyone strikes you on the right cheek, turn to him the other also.... You have heard that it was said, "You shall love your neighbor and hate your enemy." But I say to you, Love your enemies and pray for those who persecute you, so that you may be the sons of your Father who is in heaven; for he makes his sun rise on the evil and on the good, and sends rain on the just and on the unjust. For if you love those who love you, what reward have you? Do not even the tax collectors do the same? And if you salute only your brethren, what more are you doing than others? Do not even the Gentiles do the same? You, therefore, must be perfect, as your heavenly Father is perfect. (Mt 5:43–48)

Christian virtue is to go beyond the paradigms of human logic. To forgive and to love one's enemies is a divine work: "You, therefore, must be perfect, as your heavenly Father is perfect." "Be merciful, even as your Father is merciful" (Lk 6:36).

Jesus has left the Church, as his precious legacy, the power to forgive sins. In the sacraments, the Christian experiences the forgiveness of his sins and receives the grace to strengthen his resolve to pardon and love his enemies:

After his Resurrection, Christ sent his apostles "so that repentance and forgiveness of sins should be preached in his name to all nations" (Lk 24:47). The apostles and their successors carry out this "ministry of reconciliation" (2 Cor 5:18), not only by announcing to men God's forgiveness merited for us by Christ, and calling them to conversion and faith; but also by communicating to them the forgiveness of sins in Baptism, and reconciling them with God and with the Church through the power of the keys, received from Christ." (CCC, 981)

The sacrament of penance or reconciliation belongs, like the Eucharist, to the very identity of the pilgrim Church on earth, and is a privileged event of instruction in faith:

It is called the *sacrament of reconciliation,* because it imparts to the sinner the love of God who reconciles: "be reconciled to God." He who lives by God's merciful love is ready to respond to the Lord's call: "Go; first be reconciled to your brother." (CCC, 1424)

The sacrament of penance or reconciliation is a powerful tool for training in virtue and holiness: "You shall be holy, for I the Lord your God am holy" (Lv 19:2). "But as he who called you is holy, be holy yourselves in all your conduct" (1 Pet 1:15). The liturgy of the Eucharist has us pray every day to the Father using the prayer that Jesus taught us: "Our Father...forgive us our trespasses, as we forgive those who trespass against us." The holy educators like Saint John Bosco did not use this sacrament to humiliate and mortify, but made of it a stage of progress in virtue through the joyful experience of the infinite mercy of the heart of God.

The Jubilee is the favorable time to experience with greater intensity and fervor the joy of receiving pardon from God and of giving it with generosity and liberality to our neighbor.

Jesus Reveals the Father Rich in Mercy

"No one has ever seen God; the only Son, who is in the bosom of the Father, he has made him known" (Jn 1:18). The core of Jesus' message was the revelation of God. Jesus reveals and communicates the Father. At the same time he reveals himself as the Father's Son and reveals and communicates the Holy Spirit, the divine love. Indeed, he himself is the definitive revelation of God to the human race. In Jesus Christ, the ineffable God becomes sayable. If the word of God had once resounded partially in the Old Testament (not to mention the precious fragments of the word outside the Jewish biblical tradition), with Jesus the Word of God finds its full human expressive power: "In many and various ways God spoke of old to our fathers by the prophets; but in these last days he has spoken to us by a Son, whom he has appointed the heir of all things, through whom also he created the world. He... uphold[s] the universe by his word of power" (Heb 1:1–3).

Saint John confirms this: "And the Word became flesh and dwelt among us, full of grace and truth; we have beheld his glory, glory as of the only Son of the Father" (Jn 1:14). The Incarnation is the event that has manifested in all its completeness the ineffable mystery of God, of his life of charity, and of his loving openness toward the world and all of humankind. Jesus says "He who has seen me has seen the Father" (Jn 14:9). Jesus has good reason to exclaim in his prayer to the Father, "I have manifested thy name to... men" (Jn 17:6). Jesus is truly the Father's exegete. He says affectionately to his disciples, "I have called you friends, for all that I have heard from my Father I have made known to you" (Jn 15:15).

The horizon of Jesus' earthly life is not so much the plain of Galilee or the hill country around Jerusalem as the embrace of the Father who is in heaven. Likewise, Jesus' true family is communion with the Father, whom he calls "my Father who is in heaven" (Mt 16:17).

Jesus says and does everything in the name of the Father: "Truly, truly, I say to you, the Son can do nothing of his own accord, but only what he sees the Father doing; for whatever he does, that the Son does likewise" (Jn 5:19). "The Father loves the Son, and has given all things into his hand" (Jn 3:35).

Philip once asked Jesus to show him the Father. Jesus answered him in these words:

Have I been with you for so long, and yet you do not
know me, Philip? He who has seen me has seen the Father; how can you say, "Show us the Father?" Do you not
believe that I am in the Father and the Father in me? The
words that I say to you I do not speak on my own authority; but the Father who dwells in me does his works.
Believe me that I am in the Father and the Father in me;
or else believe me for the sake of the works themselves.
(Jn 14:9–11)

The most important stages in Jesus' earthly apostolate are
marked by the Father's presence and by his loving words to
the Son. When Jesus is baptized in the Jordan, "a voice came
from heaven, 'Thou art my beloved Son; with thee I am well
pleased' " (Mk 1:11). The same feelings of predilection are expressed when Jesus is transfigured on "a high mountain" (Mt
17:1). "He was still speaking, when lo, a bright cloud over-
shadowed them, and a voice from the cloud said, 'This is my
beloved Son, with whom I am well pleased; listen to him' " (Mt
17:5). At the end of his life, on his cross of torment, Jesus aban-
dons himself with confidence to the Father's charity: "Father,
into thy hands I commit my Spirit" (Lk 23:46).

There is no time in his life or place in his earthly pilgrimage
where Jesus is outside the Father. He is always in the bosom of
the Father: "The Father is in me, and I am in the Father." "I
and the Father are one" (Jn 10:30).

The Father whom Jesus reveals is not the master who op-
presses, punishes, and humiliates. Rather, he is a kind, merciful,
and provident father. He is a father who loves and protects the
little ones: "So it is not the will of my Father who is in heaven
that one of these little ones should perish" (Mt 18:14). He is
a Father who even leaves his children free to depart from him
and to squander the inheritance that is his gift to them. He is
a Father who can wait for the conversion of his wayward son
and who welcomes him back without scolding and punishing
him. Indeed, the Father rewards him with pardon and with a
big welcome home party overflowing with joy. And when the
elder son, who is good and faithful, does not understand the

reason for such limitless indulgence, the Father speaks to him with affection and understanding: "It was fitting to make merry and be glad, for this your brother was dead, and is alive; he was lost, and is found" (Lk 15:32).

Jesus proclaims a Father who considers all men his children and who "makes his sun rise on the evil and the good" (Mt 6:45).

Moreover, God's goodness is nothing but the supreme fulfillment of the often limited goodness of men. Jesus puts it this way:

> Or what man of you, if his son asks him for bread, will give him a stone? Or if he asks for a fish, will give him a serpent? If you, then, who are evil, know how to give good gifts to your children, how much more will your father who is in heaven give good things to those who ask him? (Mt 7:9–11)

For this reason, the Father's tenderness is a model to imitate and to practice: "Be merciful, even as your Father is merciful" (Lk 6:36).

Jesus' call to be merciful is very timely in a world, such as ours today, that seems to have forgotten the meaning of mercy, compassion, and forgiveness. In his encyclical *Dives in misericordia* (1980), John Paul II says that "today's mentality, perhaps even more than that of man in the past, seems to be opposed to the God of mercy. It also tends to cast out of life and to remove from man's heart the very idea of mercy. The word and the concept of mercy seem to make man uncomfortable" (*DM*, 2).

These words are always timely. There is urgent need today for a reevangelization of God's mercy toward contemporary humanity, which increasingly recognizes itself in the figure of the prodigal son of the parable. The mercy of the Father, more than a manifestation of justice, is an unshakable faithfulness to his love for his sinful son: "the love that flows from the very essence of paternity in a certain sense obliges the Father to be concerned from the dignity of the son" (*DM*, 6).

Jesus Faces His Passion and Death

The Suffering Servant

We have already seen that Jesus had an intense apostolate of healing, comforting, and encouraging all who were in need: "Come to me, all who labor and are heavy laden, and I will give you rest" (Mt 11:28). In order to restore joy and consolation to parents and relatives who were distressed by the death of their loved ones, he also worked miracles of resurrection: he raised the daughter of Jairus, the head of the synagogue (see Lk 8:40–56), the only son of the widow of Naim (see Lk 7:11–17), and his friend Lazarus, the brother of Mary and Martha, who had been dead for four days and was already beginning to stink (Jn 11:1–45).

The miracles that Jesus worked were only a sign of the irruption of the kingdom of God into history. For Jesus did not eliminate suffering and death from human existence. He announced this goal as an eschatological reality, a reality belonging to the end times, when "death shall be no more, neither shall there be mourning nor crying nor pain any more, for the former things have passed away" (Rev 21:4). Suffering and death still remain in human history, like sentinels on the alert, but Jesus gives them a profound, salvific meaning. Although Jesus relieved the suffering of others, he himself did not avoid suffering and death. On the contrary, he shared perfectly our human nature and thus knowingly and voluntarily made himself vulnerable to the traumatic experience of suffering and death. He was deeply troubled and burst into tears at the death of Lazarus (see Jn 11:35), just as in the garden of Gethsemani he was seized with fear, sadness, and anguish that made him sweat blood in the face of his imminent passion and death (see Mk 14:33; Mt 26:37; Lk 22:44). This behavior provoked both the incomprehension of the disciples, who abandoned him in his passion, and the ironic mockery of his enemies: "He saved others; he cannot save himself. Let the Christ, the King of Israel, come down now from the cross, that we may see and believe" (Mk 15:31–32).

Having seen their master's great power as a wonderworker,

the disciples could not accept a weak and suffering Jesus. And yet, after Peter's confession at Caesarea Philippi, "Jesus began to show his disciples that he must go to Jerusalem and suffer many things from the elders and chief priests and scribes, and be killed, and on the third day be raised" (Mt 16:21).

Suffering and death are present in the experience of every one, for each of us is often the victim of injustice and wickedness. Jesus entered into solidarity with those who suffer under such situations of injustice, and he gave them new value with his grace. Suffering and death are part not only of Jesus' earthly destiny, but of Christian identity itself. They are the prerequisite for the reward of eternal life:

> Blessed are those who mourn, for they shall be comforted.
> ...Blessed are you when men revile you and persecute you and utter all kinds of evil against you falsely on my account. Rejoice and be glad, for your reward is great in heaven, for so men persecuted the prophets who were before you. (Mt 5:4, 11–12)

When we follow Jesus, we experience the cross before receiving the prize:

> If any man would come after me, let him deny himself and take up his cross daily and follow me. For whoever would save his life will lose it; and whoever loses his life for my sake, he will save it. (Lk 9:23–24)

The suffering meant here is redemptive, like that of the "Servant of YHWH," the mysterious figure who anticipates in a remarkable way the paschal mystery of Jesus. The "Servant of YHWH" offered his back to those who whipped him and his cheek to those who plucked out his beard. Nor did he hide his face from insults (see Is 50:6). He thus became "a man of sorrows, and acquainted with grief" (Is 53:3). "Surely he has borne our griefs and carried our sorrows....He was wounded for our transgressions, he was bruised for our iniquities; upon him was the chastisement that made us whole, and with his stripes we are healed" (Is 53:4–5). He was "stricken for the transgression of [his] people ... although he had done no violence, and there was no deceit in his mouth" (Is 53:8–9). God rewards this innocent suffering with endless triumph. To the amazement of all the peoples and their kings the Servant "shall prosper, he shall be exalted and lifted up, and shall be very high" (Is 52:13). His triumph will also have a saving value for all people: "after his affliction, he will see the light ... the righteous one, my servant, shall make many righteous" (Is 53:11).

The Letter to the Hebrews interprets Jesus' paschal mystery in the light of the Servant:

> In the days of his flesh, Jesus offered up prayers and supplications with loud cries and tears, to him who was able to save him from death, and he was heard for his godly fear. Although he was a Son, he learned obedience through what he suffered; and being made perfect he became the source of eternal salvation to all who obey him. (Heb 5:7–9)

Jesus transforms suffering into an instrument of salvation. Obedience to the Father in the acceptance of suffering was the cause of salvation for all humankind.

In a (probably pre-Pauline) hymn in the Letter to the Philippians, Saint Paul says that Jesus, "though he was in the form of God ... emptied himself, taking the form of a servant, being born in the likeness of men. And being found in human form he humbled himself and became obedient unto death, even death on a cross. Therefore God has highly exalted him" (see Phil 2:5–11). Obedience and suffering become the cause of glorification and redemptive exaltation.

Jesus, the new Adam, the new man, through his obedient acceptance of suffering and death, restores to the Father a renewed humanity, while giving humanity the new hope of being happiness in a life without suffering and death: "God, who is rich in mercy, out of the great love with which he loved us, even when we were dead through our trespasses, made us alive together with Christ" (Eph 2:4–5).

Suffering Is Vanquished by Love

"I rejoice in my sufferings" (Col 1:24).

Like Jesus, the Christian does not face the mystery of suffering, illness, and death with an attitude of refusal, incomprehension, or passive resignation, but with a readiness to welcome what comes. For he knows that he participates by faith in Jesus' paschal mystery, that is, in his passion, death, and resurrection. Illness does not plunge the Christian into listlessness and sterility, but motivates him to participate and share actively in the redemption. The Christian can pass from the mute dismay of the knowledge of pain, to the suffering lament of acceptance, to the understanding of pain as redemptive and salvific. The Christian's pain thus becomes "salvific." Saint Paul says: "Now I rejoice in my sufferings for your sake, and in my flesh I complete what is lacking in Christ's afflictions for the sake of his body, that is, the Church" (Col 1:24).

Christ's redemption is complete, but it remains always open to the participation of the faithful who appropriate its saving effectiveness. The paschal mystery of Christ contains all the mysteries of man's suffering and redemption. Participating in Jesus' paschal mystery, the Christian finds his true definition as man: he is a "being for life," not for death. The sick and the suffering are not useless outcasts, but living members of the community of the Church, which therefore welcomes, assists, cares for, and comforts them. By uniting their sufferings to those of Christ, the sick become intercessors before God on behalf of the Church.

Even their death, when they accept it as an act of obedience to the Father, takes on meaning as a trustful offering to the God of love and of life. Death becomes an act of love, not in the sense of a sentimental outpouring, but in the awareness of being on the cross together with Jesus. Saint Thérèse of Lisieux said: "Our Lord died on the cross, in anguish, yet this is the loveliest death for love.... To die for love is not to die full of enthusiasm. I confess to you sincerely, it seems that this is what I am experiencing" (*Last conversations, yellow notebook*, 4 July, 2).

Jesus Shares Our Death

Although not found in the Niceno-Constantinopolitan Creed, the so-called *descensus ad inferos* (descent into hell) is attested in symbols of faith dating as far back as the fourth century. The paschal mystery includes not just the crucifixion, but also Jesus' death and descent into hell. "For as Jonah was three days and three nights in the belly of the whale, so will the Son of man be three days and three nights in the heart of the earth" (Mt 12:40). The sign of Jonah is the sign of Jesus' genuine passion and death. Just as Jonah had been in the dark belly of the fish, Jesus experiences the three-day period of his death in the dark entrails of the kingdom of the dead, the kingdom of uttermost dereliction and solitude. Jesus' solidarity with the dead is itself an offer of salvation to humanity, which is mortal both because of its ephemeral fragility and because of its sins. Jesus himself had said it: "Truly, truly, I say to you, the hour is coming, and now is, when the dead will hear the voice of the Son of God, and those who hear will live" (Jn 5:25). Thanks to Jesus, death takes on another meaning: once a prison of desperation, it now becomes a way of redemption.

Contemporary man, who knows so well the culture of death and the underworld, may be able to interiorize better Jesus' liberating solidarity. Even the Son of man descended into the abyss of utter abandonment, not to be trapped forever in it, but to offer a way out. Jesus' descent is an offer of an exodus and an exit: it is the hand that the new Adam stretches out to all the dead sons of man in their solitude and abandonment. It is the help given to all to escape from a destiny of meaninglessness and eternal solitude. Jesus, offering his salvation, transforms an existential situation of extreme a-spirituality into an opportunity for charity and salvation. Holy Saturday thus becomes salvation, ransom, and redemption of all the Fridays of passion and death of each and every human being.

Chapter 6

The Resurrection
of Jesus

The eucharistic prayer, which is the center and source of the Church's life, is buoyed up by its faith-filled certainty that the risen Christ is really present in the species of bread and wine. It is not for nothing that after the consecration the assembly acclaims full of enthusiasm and hope: "Dying you destroyed our death, rising you restored our life, Lord Jesus, come in glory." The golden thread that has bound together twenty centuries of Christianity in faith and hope is the event of Jesus' resurrection.

The resurrection is the crowning of history and the confirmation that man's salvation is not a utopia, but a reality. As a decisive victory over every evil and every human limitation, and as a condition and first-fruits of our resurrection, it gives a decisive impulse to the Christian's engagement in the world and to his hope for the future.

But how can we speak of the resurrection today? We shall organize the exposition around the following points. First of all, we will draw attention to the enthusiasm of the first Christian proclamation of the resurrection, as the event at the origin of proclamation. Immediately afterward, we will present the Gospel narration of the resurrection, underscoring its reality and justifying its historical reliability.

We then offer several ideas concerning the meaning of the resurrection "in itself" and "for us." We fill this out with a catechetical interpretation of the resurrection in Eastern icons and in a manifestation of popular piety. We conclude with an outline of paschal spirituality, as a Via Lucis that follows on the Via Crucis.

The Resurrection: The Mystery at the Source of the Christian Proclamation

From the very beginning, Jesus' resurrection has been the basis of Christian faith and the essential content of Christian preaching. The first Christians spoke of it with involvement and feeling, never with detachment. Among the first "confessions" of the baptismal and the eucharistic liturgies there are formulas pertaining to the resurrection that proclaim in a straightforward, enthusiastic way that Jesus has died and risen:

> We believe that Jesus died and rose again. (1 Thess 4:14)

> We ... believe in him that raised from the dead Jesus our Lord, who was put to death for our trespasses and raised for our justification. (Rom 4:24–25; see also Rom 8:32, 34; Gal 1:4; 2:30; Eph 5:2, 25)

In addition to the prophecies regarding the Davidic descent of the coming Messiah and his working of miracles, his death and resurrection-glorification were the essential elements of the apostolic kerygma (see Acts 2:14–39; 3:13–26; 4:10–12; 5:30–32; 10:36–43; 13:17–41). This is also true of the Church's catechesis today:

> The Resurrection of Jesus is the crowning truth of our faith in Christ, a faith believed and lived as the central truth by the first Christian community; handed on as fundamental by Tradition; established by the documents of the New Testament; and preached as an essential part of the Paschal mystery along with the Cross." (CCC, 638; see 539–658)

The Apostle Paul considered the resurrection to be the keystone of the mystery of Christ, the absolute criterion of the truth of his Gospel. The believers at Corinth harbored doubts about the reality of the resurrection. To them he wrote with great sincerity: "If Christ has not been raised, then our preaching is in vain. We are even found to be misrepresenting God, because we testified of God that he raised Christ, whom he did not raise if it is true that the dead are not raised" (1 Cor 15:14–15).

In order to justify the reality and truth of this event, Paul cites a precious fragment of the most ancient handbook of Christian preaching or catechesis (datable around 40 A.D.). This fragment is centered entirely on Jesus' death and resurrection. Referring to the "gospel" that he had received at the time of his conversion and had then transmitted to the Corinthians, Paul says, "I delivered to you as of first importance what I also received, that Christ died for our sins in accordance with the scriptures, that he was buried, that he was raised on the third day in accordance with the scriptures" (1 Cor 15:3–4). Paul continues: "And . . . he appeared to Cephas, then to the twelve. Then he appeared to more than five hundred brethren at one time, most of whom are still alive, though some have fallen asleep. Then he appeared to James, then to all the apostles. Last of all, as to one untimely born, he appeared also to me" (1 Cor 15:5–8).

In this passage, Paul refers to the resurrection using the Greek verb *egégertai* ("he has been raised": the perfect passive indicates an event of the past that also continues in the present) together with two pieces of information. The first, "the third day," is chronological, but it has a theological aspect. Jesus' death, though real (see the sharp "he died and was buried"), did not cause the ruinous decomposition of the body, as had happened to Lazarus, whose body already stank after four days (see Jn 11:39). Jesus really died, but death did not have a final victory over him, because it was defeated by the resurrection.

The other detail has to do with the scriptural basis of the event: "according to the scriptures." The reference is to allusions from the Old Testament (see Dt 32:39; 1 Sam 2:6; Is 38:16; Hos 6:2; Jonah 2:7; Ps 16:10; 30:3–4). For the Hebrew mentality, recourse to Scripture had more value as testimony than even the personal experience of the disciples.

In order to corroborate the reality of Jesus' resurrection, Paul speaks of appearances of the risen one, using the verb *ophthe* ("was seen," "appeared"). This does not mean dreams or subjective visions (see Acts 16:9), but real perceptions outside of the subject. The Apostle lists the witnesses of the risen one, whom he subdivides into six categories chosen among the most important and authoritative:

1. Cephas or Simon Peter, the head of the Apostles (see Lk 24:34);

2. the twelve, the technical term to indicate the college of the twelve Apostles in the strict sense, independently of the exact number of those present at the apparitions (see Lk 24:36–43; Jn 20:19–23);

3. more than five hundred brethren: these are men and women, most of whom were still living, who belonged to the first courageous Christian communities. They were the object of the Apostles' particular attention and truthful witnesses of Jesus' appearances (see 1 Cor 15:6);

4. James, called "the less" (Mk 15:40), numbered among the relatives or "brothers" of Jesus (see Gal 1:19; Mk 6:3). This James had a particular prestige because he headed the Christian community of Jerusalem (Acts 21:18–19; Gal 2:9);

5. all the apostles: meant here is the apostolic college extended to include those disciples who through the manifestation of the risen Lord had received the mission to preach the Gospel and the resurrection (see 1 Cor 15:7; Rom 1:5);

6. Paul, the witness of the risen Jesus who appeared to him on the road to Damascus (see Acts 9:3–7; 22:6–21; 26:12–18).

The Apostle makes no explicit mention of the appearances to the women (see Jn 20:1–2; Lk 24:1–10), probably because in the Hebrew culture of the time their testimony did not have legal value.

The Resurrection: Source of Understanding the Mystery of Jesus

It is a noteworthy fact that the four Gospels are very sober in presenting the event of the resurrection of Jesus, which came upon the disciples in a situation of discouragement, disappointment, and anxiety caused by their master's ignominious end. Sadness had replaced the enthusiasm aroused by the transfiguration (Mk 9:2–10; Mt 17:1–9; Lk 9:28–36) and the miracles of resurrection, of which Peter, James, and John, as well as the other disciples and the crowd, had been eyewitnesses. Before his passion and death, Jesus had raised the daughter of Jairus, head of the synagogue (Mk 5:21–24, 35–43; Mt 9:18–19, 23–26; Lk 8:40–42, 49–56), the son of the widow of Naim (Lk 7:11–17), and Lazarus of Bethany, the brother of Mary and Martha (Jn 11:1–45). He had also explicitly foretold that he would rise again on the third day after his death (see Mk 8:31, 9:31, 10:34).

Nevertheless, Jesus' resurrection did not seem to fit the understanding and expectations of the disciples (see Mk 9:10). His death had caused a grief so deep that it left no hope. In order to regain their trust, Jesus had to undertake a long pedagogy in which he met the disciples and proved that he had really risen, viz., by letting Thomas touch him (see Jn 20:27), by walking (see Lk 24:15) and eating with them (see Lk 24:42–43; Jn 21:10–12).

After his resurrection, Jesus frequently upbraids the disciples for their astonishment and their unbelief: "O foolish men, and slow of heart to believe all that the prophets have spoken. Was it not necessary that the Christ should suffer these things and enter into his glory?" (Lk 24:25–26). "Why are you troubled, and why do questionings arise in your heart?" (Lk 24:38).

A good example of this is the episode of the disciples from Emmaus who depart Jerusalem sad and disappointed because of the shipwreck of their hopes of freedom: "We had hoped that he was the one to redeem Israel. Yes, and besides all this, it is now the third day since this happened" (Lk 24:19–21). Jesus appears to them and exegetes his messianic action in the light of the promises of the Old Testament: "Beginning with Moses and all the prophets, he interpreted to them in all the scriptures the things concerning himself" (Lk 24:27).

It is thus only on Easter that the disciples come to understand fully the mystery of their master. It is true that even before that they had already seen him as the prophet with authority, the mighty wonderworker, the promised Messiah. But the event of the passion and death had confused them and had even led them to deny him. Peter, who had confessed that Jesus was "the Christ, the Son of the living God" (Mt 16:16), admits that he no longer recognizes the imprisoned and humiliated Jesus: "I do not know the man" (Mt 26:72).

It is therefore the marvelous and unexpected event of the resurrection that enables the disciples truly to understand Jesus. Easter sheds light on the authentic reality of Jesus' earthly history. This allows the disciples to pass from a superficial and incomplete recognition of Jesus to the convinced confession and tireless proclamation that leads them to give up their own lives in martyrdom. It is, in fact, the resurrection that restores to Peter and the disciples their faith and enthusiasm in Jesus, and which thus makes them tenacious and persevering messengers who spread his Gospel of salvation.

What the Resurrection Is Not: Reanimation, Immortality of the Soul, Reincarnation, or the Memory of the Dead Master

The resurrection is part of the "paschal mystery," a very rich saving event that includes Jesus' death (Good Friday), his *descensus ad inferos* (Holy Saturday), and his glorification. This glorification in turn comprises the resurrection (Easter Sunday), the ascension (forty days after Easter), and Pentecost (fifty days after Easter). The Fathers called the period from Easter to Pentecost a single great Sunday.

The New Testament refers to the event of the resurrection with other terms, such as exaltation, glorification, ascension, cosmic lordship, entry into the heavenly sanctuary (see Heb 9:11–12), presence ("Jesus lives," 2 Cor 13:4; Rom 14:9). The language of resurrection prevailed because it was the clearest and most complete way of talking about the return to life of the one who had been dead.

The resurrection is not a reanimation, that is, a simple return to earthly life, to be followed by a second death. This is the case with Jairus's daughter, the son of the widow of Naim, and Lazarus. These miracles, although they recalled dead persons to life, restored their body to ordinary human life in space and time. For this reason they had to die a second death (see CCC, 646).

The resurrection is not simply the immortality of the soul, as in a fairly widespread Gnostic understanding at the time of Christianity. In that case, it would be a sort of "half resurrection," as Tertullian would say (De resurrectione, 2). The resurrection has to do with the entrance of Jesus' body, and thus his entire humanity, into unending life. The relationship between the empty tomb and Jesus' resurrection is underscored by "two men...in dazzling apparel" (Lk 24:4) who say to the women visiting the tomb, "Why do you seek the living among the dead" (Lk 24:5).

Nor is the resurrection a reincarnation (samsara) such as Hindus and Buddhists believe in. These religions speak of man's rebirth or new fall into a new earthly existence through an unlimited series of passages or transmigrations of the soul from one body to the other.

Nor is the resurrection the simple recollection of Jesus and his teaching, as if this teaching caused the conviction in the disciples' mind that he was present after his death. The resurrection is not a psychological creation of the disciples. Rather, it is a concrete event that, even before it concerns his disciples, essentially concerned Jesus and the entrance of his mortal body into eternal life.

This event was considered to be a real fact by the first Christian community: "The Lord is risen indeed, and has appeared to Simon" (Lk 24:34). In other words, it was the encounter with the risen Jesus that caused the disciples to believe in the resurrection, and not vice versa. The resurrection was not the consequence, but the cause of the disciples' faith.

The resurrection was not something that the disciples made up because of fraud (as the chief priests and the Pharisees believed; see Mt 27:62–65), hallucination (according to outmoded rationalistic interpretations), or conversion to Jesus' teachings after Easter independently of the appearances and the empty tomb (according to a contemporary line of interpretation). All these suppositions would require low intrigue and would make the resurrection a mere psychological reminiscence of Jesus' teaching. This goes against the reality of the facts. After Jesus' death, the disciples were sad, frightened, incredulous, hard-hearted, doubtful (Lk 24:18; Mk 16:14; Mt 28:17; Lk 24:37). Only a great event could have changed them, giving them back their original enthusiasm for Jesus and following him.

The Resurrection Is a Transcendent, but Real Event

The resurrection indicates the fact that Jesus was restored, together with his humanity, to God's glorious, full, and immortal life. For this reason, his risen body, while maintaining its identity and human reality, was rendered capable of living forever in God. The body is gloriously transfigured; it becomes, as Saint Paul says, a "pneumatic" body (spiritual: 1 Cor 15:44) in the strong sense of a body entirely pervaded by the vital breath of God's creator Spirit, who transforms it from corruption to incorruption, from ignominy to glory, from weakness to strength (1 Cor 14:42–43), from mortality to immortality (1 Cor 15:53–54).

We may ask in what sense an event of this kind can be considered historical. Applying our standards of historical authenticity, we can state that the resurrection is a historical event, because the various writings of the New Testament provide ample and consistent evidence concerning it. The resurrection is, after all, the high point of the four Gospels and the thread linking together the Church's preaching, from that of Peter on the first Pentecost to our days.

Furthermore, to affirm the historicity of the resurrection means to insist that it is an event that truly happened. Let us clarify that the resurrection, insofar as it is an instantaneous passage of Jesus' humanity from death to the divine life of the Trinity, is an essentially transcendent and metahistorical event (see CCC, 647). However, it remains solidly and surely linked to history through the recognition of the empty tomb and of the reality of the appearances, which are a mysterious encounter between God's transcendence and man's immanence, between eternity and time.

Given that it is intrinsically "from above," the fact that the risen Lord allows himself to be seen is a gift of grace. This may explain the rather odd circumstance that the women and the disciples do not immediately recognize the risen Christ. It is not the Magdalene, or the disciples of Emmaus, or the Apostles who recognize Jesus; rather, it is Jesus who gives them the grace to see and recognize him.

Nevertheless, the resurrection has an obvious historical framework, a side turned toward history. Consequently, it is attested to in the sources, especially through the appearances. With his appearances, Jesus "touches" history. And this "contact" can therefore be documented. This is not, however, an immediate, but a mediate historicity. The Gospels do not bear witness to the resurrection as it happened at a certain point in time: only the apocryphal Gospel of Peter dares to offer a crude presentation of the moment of Jesus' resurrection, describing an enormous phantom that rises up to heaven. What history immediately grasps is the faith of the disciples in the risen Christ on the basis of two concrete facts: the empty tomb and the cycle of the appearances.

Limiting ourselves to the Gospel tradition, we can distinguish between two types of appearance narratives. On the one hand, there are appearances to private individuals, which do not occur according to a fixed pattern (appearances to the women: Mt 28:9ff.; to Mary Magdalene: Jn 20:11–18; to the disciples of Emmaus: Lk 24:13–35). On the other hand, there are official appearances to the Apostles (see Mt 28:16–20; Mk 16:14–18, 19–20; Lk 24:36–49; Jn 20:19–23, 24–29). These appearances have a basically fixed pattern that includes Jesus' appearance and greeting, the disciples' incredulous reaction, Jesus' reproof, the proof of his reality and identity, and the conferral of mission.

The Many Meanings of the Resurrection

One may well ask what is the significance of this event, what is the word that God intends to say to us in the unusual and tremendous event of his Son's resurrection. What is the significance of the resurrection for Jesus and what is its value for us? In other words, what is the "in itself" and the "for us" of the resurrection?

The Christological and Trinitarian Meaning of the Resurrection

In the first place, the resurrection is God the Father's answer to the condemnation and execution that men inflicted on Jesus (see Acts 2:23–24; 3:13–15; 4:10–12; 5:30–31; 10:39–40; 13:28–30). The resurrection reveals Jesus to be "Lord and Christ" (Acts 2:36), "Lord and God" (Jn 20:28), "Son of God" (Acts 13:33). It confirms the divinity of Jesus, who, as the incarnate Son of God, returns to the loving communion of the Father along with his risen humanity. Jesus is truly the "resurrection and the life" (Jn 11:25). In the words of the *Catechism of the Catholic Church*, "The Resurrection of the crucified one shows that he was truly 'I Am,' the Son of God and God himself" (*CCC*, 653).

In the second place, the resurrection completes the supreme revelation of God as Trinity: of the Father, who glorifies the Son by raising him and exalting him to his, the Father's, right hand; of the Son, who by his redeeming sacrifice merits this exaltation to the right hand of the Father; of the Holy Spirit, who proves himself to be the Spirit of life and resurrection: "Christ ... being put to death in the flesh but made alive in the spirit" (1 Pet 3:18).

The resurrection means that the humanity of the Son is glorified and enters into the communion of the triune God. In the Incarnation, this humanity had been assumed by the divine person of the Word. With the resurrection, the humanity attains the fullness of this highest relation with God, in that it lives by the very life of the Trinity itself. The glorious humanity of the Son is present in the trinitarian communion.

Jesus' resurrection marked, in fact, the beginning of the final and definitive events of salvation. In the risen Jesus the *eschaton* is already present, pregnant with new qualities of divine life.

The Meaning of the Resurrection "For Us"

In addition to its christological and trinitarian significance, the resurrection has a fundamental soteriological meaning: "If you confess with your lips that Jesus is Lord and believe in your heart that God raised him from the dead, you will be saved" (Rom 10:9). The resurrection does not merely precede the resurrections to come as their first-fruits, but also makes them possible.

The resurrection is the event that repairs the friendship between God and man in which the divine life streams abundantly into the humanity of Christ (objective redemption) and, through him, into all of humanity (subjective redemption). This influx of the risen Christ is not merely exemplary or intentional, but real and efficacious. Because he is risen, he has the spiritual power to transform men according to his image in order to make them sons of the Father.

Jesus' resurrection is the realization of the new humanity set free from the slavery of sin and its consequences, such as death and physical, moral, and psychological evil. The risen Jesus is the new man who involves the whole of humanity in this destiny of newness. A significant example of the beneficent effects of the presence of the risen Christ for needy man is the episode of the healing of the lame man who begged near the Beautiful Gate of the temple in Jerusalem. Not having any money, Peter gave him the most valuable thing he had, the gift of the risen Christ: "I have no silver and gold, but I give you what I have; in the name of Jesus Christ of Nazareth, walk. And he took him by the right hand and raised him up; and immediately his feet and ankles were made strong. And leaping up he stood and walked" (Acts 3:6–8).

Peter's act of lifting up the cripple and restoring his physical health and spiritual joy is a sign of the new humanity inaugurated and realized by the resurrection of Jesus.

The resurrection is also the fulfillment of man's hope for

immortality and transcendence. In every human being we find this "transcendental hope," which is a "yes" to his own eternal existence and the definitiveness of his personal realization.

Jesus' resurrection is the experience of encountering him in the breaking of the bread, in eucharistic communion. He manifested himself to the disciples of Emmaus "in the breaking of the bread" (Lk 24:35). In history, the Eucharist is not only the memorial of the death and resurrection of Jesus, but is also real participation in the divine life of the risen Christ. In the Eucharist, the sacrament of the continuous saving presence of the risen Lord in history, our saving encounter with him is realized. After his resurrection, Jesus had said, "Lo, I am with you always, to the close of the age" (Mt 28:20). The risen Christ is present in his mystical body and in his eucharistic body.

Jesus' resurrection is also an experience of vocation and mission. For the disciples, the resurrection was the event of their "reconvocation" by Jesus following upon their dispersion at the time of Jesus's passion and death. For forty days, from Easter to the ascension, Jesus appeared to his disciples, calling them to follow him again and giving to Peter and the other Apostles their definitive mission. He solemnly ordered Peter (three times in succession) to feed his flock: "Feed my lambs" (see Jn 21:15–19). He gave the Apostles the following command: "As the Father has sent me, even so I send you" (Jn 20:21). "All authority in heaven and on earth has been given to me. Go therefore and make disciples of all nations, baptizing them in the name of the Father and of the Son and of the Holy Spirit, teaching them to observe all that I have commanded you; and lo, I am with you always, to the close of the age" (Mt 28:18–20).

Jesus' resurrection is an experience not only of vocation and mission, but also of forgiveness. The risen Jesus gives back his friendship and forgiveness to the disciples. What is more, he confirms the Apostles in the office of forgiving the sins of humanity. He entrusts the power that he has exercised during his life on earth to his Apostles as his resurrection gift. On the evening of Easter Jesus, appearing to his disciples, gave them the power to remit sins: "Receive the Holy Spirit. If you forgive the sins of any, they are forgiven; if you retain the sins of any, they are retained" (Jn 20:22–23). For Christians, Jesus' resurrection is an experience of mercy, forgiveness, spiritual renewal, and participation in Jesus' victory over sin and death.

For the disciples, the resurrection was an experience of total conversion to Jesus. Only with the resurrection did they truly return to him in faith and full abandonment to his power and his divine presence in their midst. We have the example of Peter and Thomas: Easter gives us disciples converted once and for all to the cause of Jesus and his Gospel. Conversion, then, does not belong only to the time before Easter, but is an integral part of Easter. It is an ongoing passage from unbelief to faith, from sadness to joy, from the paralysis of fear to the enthusiasm of the mission.

Jesus' resurrection is also an event of liberation, inasmuch as it radically transforms humanity and nature, freeing them from the nets of sin, death, and suffering, whether physical, moral, or psychological. The man Jesus is restored to his integral freedom; a new lifestyle, set forth in the message of the risen Lord and his kingdom of justice, peace, and human solidarity, is born.

The resurrection really promotes woman as disciple, hearer, and messenger of the Word of God. The deep faithfulness and devotion of the women gave them the courage to go to the tomb before anyone else, the opportunity to be the first to receive the tremendous news of the resurrection, the chance to be the first to meet with the risen Lord and to bring this extraordinary news to the Apostles (see Mt 28:1–10; Lk 24:8–11). The resurrection brings about a radical revaluation of women: they are not the last, but the first to bear witness in faith to the risen Christ.

The figure of Mary Magdalen is emblematic in this regard. She encounters Jesus even before the Apostles do. In this way she becomes the first messenger of his resurrection and ascension and earns the title "apostle to the Apostles" (see *MD,* 16).

Today we ask, "Dic nobis Maria quid vidisti in via?" (Tell us, Mary, what you saw on the way).

"I have seen the tomb of the living Christ and the glory of
the risen one; the angels bearing witness, the shroud, and
the clothes. Christ my hope is risen."

We too respond to this message with enthusiasm and faith:

"We know that Christ is truly risen. O victorious king,
have mercy on us. Amen. Alleluia."

Jesus' entrustment of divine truths to women, as, for example, in the case of the Samaritan woman (see Jn 4:1–42), finds
its worthy crown in this episode.

The Icon: Proclaiming the Resurrection in Images

A synthesis of the meaning of the resurrection "for us" can be
found in the Byzantine iconographic tradition, which is also
present in the medieval West. The icon, as the believer's encounter with, and participation in, the mystery being celebrated,
shows the risen Jesus in the center. He is resplendent with glory
and surrounded by figures from the Old and New Testaments.
The glorious Christ holds in his right hand the standard of the
cross on which he suffered and died, the cross that is the source
of the redemption of all humankind. While the right hand is
raised aloft, the left extends downward to grasp the hand of
an old man and draw him out of the grave. Jesus Christ, the
new Adam, has the power to liberate the old Adam and all of
humanity from slavery to death and from the meaninglessness
of the underworld. Jesus tramples and destroys this kingdom,
which is symbolized by an old man crushed to the ground amid
the wreckage of the gates of Hades. In the icon, Jesus has cast
down these gates and scattered about death's instruments of
torture — nails, tongs, hammers....

In its essence the icon expresses the true sense of the resurrection in Christianity: the resurrection is the glorification of Jesus,
but also the glorification of man and his participation in Jesus'
victory over death. The other details of the icon enrich this
proclamation of liberation. Behind Adam, there is a long line
of men and women, such as Eve, Moses, David, and Solomon,

who also share in this redemptive event. Among others, we can make out the figure of John the Baptist. Holding a scroll, he announces with outstretched hand the coming of Jesus. The Baptist is the precursor of the Messiah no less among the dead than among the living. In sum, the Byzantine icon of the resurrection shows humankind's expectancy and its participation in the salvation brought by Jesus.

The Resurrection in Popular Piety

Of the many expressions of popular piety centered on Easter, we present one that is very widespread in certain nations. In the Philippines, the feast of Jesus' resurrection is celebrated with a popular tradition divided into two parts. The first is called the *Salubong* (meeting); the people celebrate it with two processions in the streets of the cities. The second is the celebration of the Easter Mass in Church.

The *Salubong* goes like this. Toward four o' clock on Easter morning, while it is still dark, two processions — one with the risen Jesus and one with Mary, the *mater dolorosa* — start from two different points of the city. Mary is dressed in a black veil, and she has an expression of great grief on account of her Son's death.

Both processions end up in the main square of the city, where a huge crowd gathered in devoted prayer awaits them. With coordinated movements the statues approach the arch of the "meeting," where a child dressed like an angel in a white gown intones the "Regina Caeli, Laetari, Alleluia." At this point, all the choirs send up Easter songs to the accompaniment of musical bands.

Meanwhile, the angel dressed in white takes off Mary's black veil. The Blessed Virgin, dressed in splendid golden garments, now seems to smile at seeing the risen Jesus next to her. This is the joyous meeting, the *Salubong*, of the Mother and her risen and triumphant Son. Immediately afterward, the procession enters the Church for the celebration of the Mass of Easter. Dawn has just broken and the sky is triumphantly streaked with light and blue.

This is a popular Easter catechesis containing the following important points:

1. The darkness of the night symbolizes sin and death;

2. the risen Jesus travels through the cities of the world to announce to Mary and the whole Church his triumph over sin and death;

3. the encounter with the risen one restores joy to the whole Church, which celebrates in the Eucharist the saving encounter with Jesus.

Signs of Easter Spirituality

Both in the East and the West, the concrete experience of the life of grace in the risen Lord basically includes two phases: the phase of asceticism, of struggle against sin and victory over the vices, and the phase of mysticism, of strengthening virtuous habits, of the triumph of grace and communion with God. We can speak of an itinerary with two basic stages: the lenten and the paschal stages. The Spiritual Exercises of Saint Ignatius of Loyola are a magisterial example of this itinerary. Divided into four weeks, the Exercises devote the first three weeks to conversion, to the imitation of Jesus, and to following him in the mysteries of his earthly life, especially in the participation in the mystery of his passion and death. The Exercises then devote the fourth and last week to the experience of meeting the risen Christ on Easter, the summit and fulfillment of the life of grace.

Concretely, the Exercises invite us to meditate not only on the stations of the Via Crucis, but also some of the stations of an ideal Via Lucis of resurrection, in which the Master is the risen Christ. We thus have fourteen steps taken from Scripture and the Church's tradition that recall Jesus' appearances to his mother Mary (*Spiritual Exercises,* 299), to Mary Magdalene (300), to the three Marys (301), to Peter (302), to the disciples of Emmaus (303), to the disciples in the Upper Room (304), to Thomas (305), to the seven disciples at the seashore (306), to the disciples on Mount Tabor (307), to the five hundred brethren (308), to James (309), to Joseph of Arimathea (310), to Paul (311), and to the Apostles at the ascension.

Christian preaching should insist with enthusiasm not only on the lenten experience of conversion and purification, but also on the paschal experience of communion and glorification with the risen Christ. In this sense we can legitimately speak of a spirituality of the Via Lucis that follows and crowns the tried and true traditional spirituality of the Via Crucis. This is the experience of those who aim to follow the path of the Apostles and the first disciples, who passed from the disappointment and dejection of the passion and death to the wonder and joy of the meeting the risen Lord.

The spirituality of Easter is an invitation to contemporary Christians to become better acquainted with the song of Easter, which is the song of life. It is a gratifying gift for everyone: for non-Christians, to whom is disclosed the horizon of an enchanting utopia; for Christians, to whom the land of their final harborage appears more exciting than ever; for the young, to whom the true lever of history is entrusted with confidence and hope.

Chapter 7

The Mystery of Jesus' Birth

The Biblical Data

The first Christian community followed up the joyful news of Jesus' resurrection with a meditation on the great event of the Savior's birth, which is recounted in the New Testament by the Evangelists Matthew and Luke.

After having set out the genealogy of "Jesus Christ, the son of David, the son of Abraham" (Mt 1:1), the Evangelist Matthew continues in the following vein:

> Now the birth of Jesus Christ took place in this way. When his mother Mary had been betrothed to Joseph, before they came together she was found to be with child of the Holy Spirit; and her husband Joseph, being a just man and unwilling to put her to shame, resolved to divorce her quietly. But as he considered this, behold, an angel of the Lord appeared to him in a dream, saying, "Joseph, son of David, do not fear to take Mary your wife, for that which is born of her is of the Holy Spirit; she will bear a son, and you shall call his name Jesus, for he will save his people from their sins. . . . " When Joseph woke from sleep, he did as the angel of the Lord commanded him; he took his wife, but knew her not until she had borne a son; and he called his name Jesus. . . . Jesus was born in Bethlehem of Judea in the days of Herod the king." (Mt 1:18–2:1)

Although he employs a different narrative structure, the Evangelist Luke also refers to Jesus' virginal conception from Mary by the working of the Holy Spirit. After the annunciation of the birth of John the Baptist, the Evangelist recounts the annunciation of the angel to Mary:

> Do not be afraid, Mary, for you have found favor with God. And behold, you will conceive in your womb and

106

bear a son, and you shall call his name Jesus. He will be great, and will be called the Son of the Most High; and the Lord God will give to him the throne of his father David, and he will reign over the house of Jacob forever; and of his kingdom there will be no end. And Mary said to the angel, "How can this be, since I have no husband?" And the angel said to her, "The Holy Spirit will come upon you, and the power of the Most High will overshadow you; therefore the child to be born will be called holy, the Son of God." (Lk 1:30–35)

In the second chapter, Luke also narrates with utter simplicity Jesus' birth in Bethlehem, where Mary and Joseph had gone for the census:

And while they were there, the time came for her to be delivered. And she gave birth to her first-born son and wrapped him in swaddling cloths, and laid him in a manger, because there was no place for them in the inn. (Lk 2:6–7)

The Faith of the Church

These invaluable biblical data, whose source is ultimately the Blessed Virgin Mary, was expressed synthetically by the Church's faith in the Niceno-Constantinopolitan Creed. Referring to the Son of God, the Creed confesses that "by the power of the Holy Spirit he was born of the Virgin Mary and became man" (DS, 150). The Son of God, eternally begotten of the Father before all ages, was born in time of the Virgin Mary by the working of the Holy Spirit. These affirmations unfold the contents of the very ancient Pauline text which reads: "When the time had fully come, God sent forth his Son, born of woman" (Gal 4:4). The Virgin Mary is the woman who became the mother of the incarnate Son of God.

The Church solemnly confirmed the scriptural data by proclaiming as dogma that Mary is the *Theotókos* (God-bearer) at the Council of Ephesus in 431. The Second Vatican Council corroborates this ancient item of faith in its Dogmatic Constitution on the Church: "By her faith and her obedience, she [Mary] generated on earth the same Son of the Father, not by knowing man, but under the shadow of the Holy Spirit" (*LG*, 63).

The Reality of the Virginal Conception

Jesus' virginal conception by Mary (see *CCC*, 484–511) is a mystery that we must receive and meditate upon in an attitude of obedient faith and in the conviction that "with God nothing is impossible" (Lk 1:37). The text deals with God's action in history, which he performs not to upset the laws of nature, but to remind the whole of humankind that the triune God is the Lord of history.

Without an adult faith, reason is unable to grasp the meaning of talk about Mary's "virginal motherhood" and the message it contains. The *Catechism of the Catholic Church* rightly recalls the well-known sentence of Saint Ignatius of Antioch: "Mary's virginity and giving birth, and even the Lord's death, escaped the notice of the prince of this world: these three mysteries worthy of proclamation were accomplished in God's silence" (*CCC*, 498; *Ad Eph*, 19, 1).

The reality of Jesus' virginal conception by Mary is backed up by a series of reasons that we do no more than list here:

1. the authenticity of the first two chapters of Matthew and Luke and the attestation of the fact in two sources that are independent of each other;

2. the lack of true parallels either in the biblical or in the extrabiblical domain;

3. the remarkable convergence of the data, notwithstanding the difference in narrative structure between the accounts of Matthew and Luke;

4. the awareness that the theological interpretation given by the Evangelists is not a betrayal or mythical manipulation of history, but adequately explains and sets forth the facts.

The Meaning of the "Sign"

What is the significance of this event? What is God trying to say in the "sign" of the virginal conception of his divine Son?

Down through the centuries, the Church has ceaselessly meditated on the meaning of this remarkable event, which occurs as an absolute novelty. As such it is the sign of the newness of the redemption. In the horizon of the continuity of his creation, God institutes a radical discontinuity, a pure beginning, so as to indicate the advent of his re-creation, of his kingdom.

Furthermore, the virginal conception manifests the reality of the divinity of the Son, who even as man is wholly *from* and *of* the heavenly Father. The virginal generation is the human expression of his divine origin.

The exclusion of an earthly father also suggests that God did not work through the exaltation of earthly values such as wealth, power, and sex, but through the evangelical values of poverty, humility, and virginity.

There is a mysterious correlation between Jesus' birth and his Passover. The absolute novelty of Jesus' birth is a prelude to the other marvelous novelty of his resurrection. In the Christ event the two decisive moments in man's earthly destiny are re-created from within. They become proleptic signs of the definitive realization of all things in God. And the same Spirit who raised up the humanity of the Son of God in history also raised it into the glory of Easter triumph. In this way, God overcomes man's radical limits and renews man with his marvels. The Virgin Birth and the resurrection from the dead on the third day are a single sign whose function is to represent the harmony of Jesus' human existence with his divine reality.

Jesus' birth from on high, from the Holy Spirit, is intrinsically linked with his birth from below, from the Virgin Mary. The Son's birth in time is accomplished with the free and personal collaboration of the Virgin, who becomes the Mother of the Lord (see Lk 1:43), and thus legitimately *Theotókos*. Because of her assent in obedient faith to the Word of God, Mary is much more than an "extra" in the private life of Jesus of Nazareth. Her "fiat" is an event belonging to the history of salvation.

Chapter 8

Jesus, the One and Definitive Savior of Humanity

Jesus: He Who Lives

Ever since the resurrection, the Church has openly professed her faith in Jesus Christ, the risen and living Lord. A question occasionally arises, namely, is the Christ whom the Church proclaims, the Christ of the liturgy, of popular piety, of our personal faith, of theology, catechesis, and pastoral ministry the same "historical Jesus" whom the sources record and narrate? Or is the Christ whom Christians announce today an undue stretching of the biblical Jesus? Putting it briefly: is the Christ of our faith different from the real Jesus of history, and is the Christ of the Church different from the Christ of the Bible?

If the answer were "yes," the authentic Jesus of history would not be the same person as the (inauthentic) Christ of faith. The problem before us is the "spiritual and ecclesial" understanding of Christ in the two-thousand-year life of the Church.

This problem has a typical history of its own that begins at the end of the eighteenth century in a Europe completely caught up in the enthusiasm of the Enlightenment. Certain scholars denied the "Christ of Christian dogma" as being an illegitimate construction on the part of the Church. Assuming that the Christ of the Church's faith was essentially unreliable, such scholars attempted to recover the authentic face of the historical Jesus. They produced rationalistic, fantastic, mythical, and romantic "biographies" of the founder of Christianity. When reason could no longer provide "convincing explanations," imagination, or mythical interpretation, or romantic inspiration took over. This search ran aground in an absolute skepticism which denied that Jesus had even existed. After having denied the Christ of faith and the Church's dogma, scholars denied even the historical reality of Jesus.

The reaction to this tendency was sharp, and it led to the opposite extreme. The Jesus of history was abandoned as being difficult to identify, and emphasis was now placed on the Christ of the *kérygma*. The motto was now Paul's statement in 2 Cor 5:16: "From now on, therefore, we know no one according to the flesh; even though we once knew Christ according to the flesh, we know him thus no longer." According to this point of view, Christianity did not begin so much with the history of Jesus, but with the preaching of the disciples after Easter.

We have already seen in chapter 4 that the situation has changed considerably in favor of the historical, even biographical, reliability of the New Testament sources, especially of the Gospels. This fact precludes denying or calling into question the basic continuity between the Jesus of history and the Christ proclaimed by the primitive Church's *kérygma*. Christian faith has its beginning in the historical Jesus. The Easter preaching itself refers to the historical Jesus as its foundation and justification. The significance attributed to Jesus' death comes not from the interpretation of the *kérygma,* but from Jesus himself. There is thus a personal continuity between the historical Jesus and the Christ believed by the primitive Church's faith.

Moreover, the principal facts that make up the so-called "Christ of faith" — the Christ preached by the Apostles after Easter — are events belonging and tracing back to the "historical Jesus": the preaching of the kingdom, the miracles, Jesus' awareness of being the Messiah and Son of God, the titles "Son of man," and "Son," the expression "I Am," Jesus' death on the cross, and his resurrection (see *CCC, 512*). In order to corroborate his teaching, Paul himself refers to Jesus before Easter, unmistakably identifying him with the person of the risen Lord (see 1 Cor 7:10; 9:14). Recalling the institution of the Eucharist, the Apostle makes the following statement:

For I received from the Lord what I also delivered to you, that the Lord Jesus on the night when he was betrayed took bread, and when he had given thanks, he broke it, and said, "This is my body which is for you. Do this in remembrance of me." (1 Cor 11:23–24)

We can affirm that the same continuity also exists between the Christ of faith and the Christ of dogma. Even today, the Niceno-Constantinopolitan Creed gives proof of this remarkable and unaltered continuity of faith.

We can therefore conclude this section by saying that the Christ of the Church's faith is the Jesus of history whose Incarnation, death, and resurrection are seen in their full importance for salvation. There is a continuity of person between the Jesus transmitted to us by the New Testament and the Christ proclaimed by the Church's two-thousand-year-old tradition. This Christ is not an inauthentic, distorted Christ, but a genuine Christ as understood, experienced, and expressed anew in the light of the categories of different cultures in time and space. This is why we speak of the Christ *of the Church and the Bible.* The saving history of Jesus cannot be limited to the past recorded in the Bible. It continues in the experience and the life of the Church, which in the Spirit confesses Jesus as the Living One, the risen Lord, he who is present in the Eucharist to sanctify the Church and join it on its path.

Jesus, the One Savior of the World

In *Tertio Millennio Adveniente,* Pope John Paul II says that the "general theme which many bishops and cardinals have proposed for this year [1997] is 'Jesus Christ, the only Savior of the world, yesterday and today and forever' (see Heb 13:8)" [*TMA,* 40].

This is the most important statement of our faith in Jesus Christ. It means that God's will to save all humankind has been manifested and accomplished in a unique and definitive way in the mystery of Jesus and his ecclesial community, which is the sacrament of salvation in history. Jesus is the sole source that sustains every other appeal for, and grant of, salvation present even outside Christianity. He is the sole, constitutive mediator of salvation for the whole of humankind. Only in him do humankind, history, and the cosmos find once and for all their positive meaning, do they reach total fulfillment, do they achieve purification and freedom forever from the nets of death — whether physical, psychic, social, ethical, spiritual, or cosmic. It is Jesus who has in himself, in what he did and who he is, the reasons for the absolute definitiveness of salvation. He is not one of many mediators of salvation, but the only and final mediator, the source of every other participated mediation.

The Challenge to the Saving Universality of Jesus

There are not a few factors today that make it urgent for us to understand and ground in new ways the Church's traditional faith in the universal saving value of the mystery of Jesus Christ. One such factor is a marked cultural and religious pluralism that is increasingly brought home by the large-scale migration of individuals — especially young people — and of whole families to the North and West. Another is a certain slackening and weakening of the Church's missionary outreach toward non-Christians. Yet others are the reawakening of the other religions, which are rediscovering their role as a source and guarantee of human values such as national identity and independence, or peace and universal harmony, and the fascination of a new religiosity that seems to offer an alternative in culture and lifestyle to the empty and superficial postmaterialistic existence typical of the West.

To all this we have to add the Council's reevaluation of the saving value of non-Christian religions, the demand for the inculturation of faith and "contextual" theology, and the promotion of joint interreligious dialogue, a notable expression of which was the day for peace celebrated by representatives of the world religions in Assisi on 27 October 1986.

This new cultural horizon has given rise to the establishment of a new theological discipline, the *theology of religions*, which seeks to discern the saving import of non-Christian religions — whether they be the great Oriental traditions or the so-called traditional religions — with respect to the event of Christ.

"All You Peoples, Open Your Doors to Christ" (*RMi,* 3)

The Second Vatican Council emphatically reaffirmed that Jesus is the sole, universal savior of the whole of humankind. Any faith, grace, and salvation that there may be outside of Christianity would draw their saving value substantially from the event of Jesus' death and resurrection (see *LG,* 16; *GS,* 22; *AG,* 7). The grace of Christ is the cause and the substance of the salvation of all humankind, both inside and outside the Church. Through the presence of his Spirit of holiness, Jesus remains the savior who *constitutes* and originates every salvation that there is in the world: "In fact, everything good and true that is found among them the Church considers as a preparation for the Gospel, as a gift granted by him who enlightens every man so that he may at last have life" (*LG,* 16).

Twenty five years after the conclusion of the Council, John Paul II, in his encyclical *Redemptoris Missio* (1990), invites the Church to renew its commitment to mission: "For mission renews the Church, imparts fresh vigor to Christian faith and identity, and gives new enthusiasm and new reasons to go forward. Faith strengthens when it is given away!... All peoples, open your doors to Christ" (*RMi,* 3). The encyclical sums up how the Church understands in faith the non-Christian religions today.

In the first place, it stresses that Jesus is the "only savior" of all humankind (see *RMi,* 4–11). This was the first, extremely condensed, message that the Apostles preached. Here is Saint Peter responding to the Jewish religious authorities concerning the healing of the cripple: "by the name of Jesus Christ of Nazareth, whom you crucified, whom God raised from the dead, by him this man is standing before you well.... And there is salvation in no one else, for there is no other name under heaven given among men by which we must be saved" (Acts 4:10, 12). Saint Paul likewise sees the risen Christ as the Lord: "For although there may be so-called gods in heaven or on earth — as indeed there are many 'gods' and many 'lords' — yet for us there is one God, the Father, from whom are all things, and one

Lord, Jesus Christ, through whom are all things, and through whom we exist" (1 Cor 8:5–6). The same Apostle confirms that "there is one mediator between God and man, the man Christ Jesus, who gave himself as a ransom for all" (1 Tim 2:5–6). The Apostle John also testifies to the fact that Jesus Christ is the one savior of all: "For God so loved the world that he gave his only Son, that whoever believes in him should not perish but have eternal life. For God sent the Son into the world, not to condemn the world, but that the world might be saved through him" (Jn 3:16–17).

The Pope sums up this united witness:

> Therefore, men cannot enter into communion with God except through Christ, under the action of the Spirit. Christ's unique and universal mediation, far from being an obstacle on the path toward God, is the way that God himself has established. Christ is fully aware of this fact. Although participated mediations of various kinds and orders are not positively ruled out, they nonetheless draw their meaning and value *solely* from Christ's mediation and cannot be understood as parallel and complementary. (*RMi,* 5)

The gifts of every kind, especially the spiritual treasures, that God has lavished on every people cannot be disjoined from Jesus Christ, "who is at the center of God's plan of salvation" (*RMi,* 6).

In the second place, the Pope warns against separating the eternal Word from Jesus Christ: "It is contrary to Christian faith to introduce any kind of separation between the Word and Jesus Christ. Saint John affirms clearly that the Word who 'was in the beginning' with God,' is the same who 'became flesh' (Jn 1:2, 14): Jesus is the incarnate Word, he is one indivisible person. Jesus cannot be separated from Christ" (*RMi,* 6).

Finally, the Pope urges Christians to be wary of identifying the object of the *missio ad gentes* with a program of mere socioeconomic well-being. The content of the missionary message is the very person of Jesus Christ: "The kingdom of God is not a concept, a doctrine, or a program that we can devise at will.

Rather, it is first of all *a person* who has the face and name of Jesus of Nazareth, the image of the invisible God" (*RMi,* 18).

The Will to Save All Men: God's "Secret Ways"

It is perhaps appropriate to make a further contribution to the understanding of this affirmation that is so central to the Christian faith. It is a fact that in God's plan, no one is deprived of the chance to be saved. In the New Testament, for example, it is said that the child Jesus being presented in the Temple is the "salvation which thou has prepared in the presence of all peoples, a light of revelation for the gentiles" (Lk 2:30–32; see Lk 3:6). Saint Paul asserts that God "desires all men to be saved and to come to the knowledge of the truth" (1 Tim 2:4). Saint John, for his part, says that Jesus is "propitiatory for the sins ... of the whole world" (1 Jn 2:2). Speaking of God's judgment, Saint Paul declares that the reward for the good will be the same for all without distinction: "but glory and honor and peace for every one who does good, the Jew first and also the Greek. For God shows no partiality" (Rom 2:10–11).

The primitive Church believed that the event of Christ was efficacious for the salvation not only of Christians, but for the whole of humanity without any discrimination. In the words of the Niceno-Constantinopolitan Creed, "for us men and for our salvation, he came down from heaven." The Second Vatican Council suggests that those who do not know Christ and live in other religious contexts are offered salvation by mysterious paths that are known only to God.

This "secret of God" is affirmed, for example, by the Council's document on missionary activity *Ad Gentes,* where we read as follows: "Although God, *by ways known to himself* [*viis sibi notis*], can bring to faith men who through no fault of their own do not know the Gospel ... " (*AG,* 7). These mysterious ways that are known only to God are actually obedience to one's own upright conscience, the doing of good and the avoidance of evil, adherence to the truth, and consistency between faith and life. In these cases, salvation is genuinely offered on the basis above all of practice of good, according to what Jesus says in Mt 25:31–46. In the last judgment, authentic knowledge of Jesus and salvation in him are the result of service to the needy.

Jesus, the "Sole Mediator" between God and Humanity

God's will to save all people is accomplished concretely in history by means of the unique efficacy of the mystery of Jesus' Passover. Alongside God's will to save, we must affirm with equal force that humankind's only way to salvation is the Christ event, which is seen as the fulfillment of every revelation: "In many and various ways, God spoke of old to our fathers by the prophets; but in these last days he has spoken to us by a Son, whom he appointed heir of all things, through whom also he created the universe" (Heb 1:1–2). "No one has ever seen God; the only Son, who is in the bosom of the Father, he has made him known" (Jn 1:18). The firm teaching of Saint Paul is that "there is no distinction between Jew and Greek; the same Lord is Lord of all and bestows his riches upon all who call upon him. For, 'every one who calls upon the name of the Lord will be saved'" (Rom 10:12–13).

All of humanity is thus called to salvation in Christ, who died and rose again for all. See the synthesis of all this in 1 Tim 2:4–6, where we read the following: "[God] desires all men to be saved and to come to the knowledge of the truth. For there is one God, and there is one mediator between God and men, the man Christ Jesus, who gave himself as a ransom for all."

Jesus, Absolute Distinction

At this point, two questions arise. The first has to do with the basic reason why there is an "unsurpassable qualitative difference" between Christ and other, non-Christian mediations of salvation.

The answer can be put like this. This difference is not based on a sweeping negative judgment about non-Christian religions that would, for example, underscore the religious and moral aberrations that they might contain. Nor is it based on a relatively positive consideration of them as, say, an honest human effort to reach God. For we live in a history of salvation; it began with creation and is pervaded from beginning to end by God's grace, so that the search for God is always a divine gift from above (see *LG,* 16; *AG,* 3, 7). Nor is it right to call non-Christian religions an "anonymous Christianity." After all, Christianity is personal and conscious acceptance of the mystery of Christ and immersion of one's whole being into the divine life of the Trinity through baptism.

It follows that we must look for the radical difference between Christianity and non-Christian religions in the mystery of Jesus Christ, in his historical self-revelation, and in his special presence in the Church, which is his sacrament of salvation for humanity. Jesus Christ alone is light, salvation, and grace. There is no opposition between non-Christian religions — with their sense of the holy mystery, of prayer, or morality, of good works, of ascetical effort, and of mystical graces — and Christianity. Instead there is transcendence, a qualitative leap due solely to the mystery of Jesus, which we accept, it is true by faith, but by a sufficiently well-grounded faith.

This brings us to the second question: How can a historical event that is limited in time and space rise to the dignity and value of absolute salvation? How, in other words, can the history of Jesus Christ go beyond the relativity and ambiguity belonging to it?

We can give the following summary response. Human history is, de facto, the scene of God's dialogue of salvation with man. This is the root of the undeniably positive significance of the non-Christian religions. These religions are, accordingly, not merely vain attempts on man's part, but a true, albeit partial, gift of enlightenment and grace from above. Consequently, this same history can also be a source of the elements and the indices of "historical certanty" for a possible incarnation and presence of the absolute savior. This is this basis for overcoming historical relativism and the pluralism of salvation that goes with it. History can offer, and in fact does so, the events capable of grounding faith in the absolute savior.

It follows from this that we can identify God's definitive revelation of himself in the historical event of Christ and can give reasons for accepting this self-revelation in faith. Just as history gives evidence of the multiplicity and plurality of man's saving dialogue with God, it can also give evidence of the fulfillment of this saving dialogue and the definitive event of salvation. If history already contains de facto a plurality of "hierophanies," it can also provide us with "christophany." If history can contain the myth of Babel, it can also contain the event of Pentecost, wherein all the nations are saved in Christ.

The Bases of Jesus' Claim to be the Savior of All

We can reduce to five the core bases of Jesus' claim. The convergence of these extremely well-founded indices makes evident the absolute discontinuity between Jesus and other mediators of salvation. For at the heart of it all is Jesus' own consistent, continuous, and conscious testimony throughout his earthly life that he was the sole and definitive savior of humanity who surpassed and fulfilled every previous and future law and covenant between God and man.

1. *Jesus' pre-Easter awareness of being Son and Messiah* — that is, Jesus' human awareness that he was the Son of the heavenly Father and the Messiah whom the Father had sent to save humankind — is an established fact.

2. *The paschal event of death and resurrection* is a reality that saves all people. The proclamation of the cross and resurrection as the mystery of universal redemption is the bedrock which sustains Christian faith and gives it its unique identity in relation to the other religions. The immortality of the soul and personal resurrection are the Christian answer to the doctrine of reincarnation.

3. *Christianity is the religion of the revelation of the name of God as a trinitarian communion and as love.* Jesus reveals God as "love" (1 Jn 4:8, 16). The Father loves the Son (Jn 15:9; 3:35; 14:31) and sets up his dwelling of love in the disciples (Jn 14:21–23). Love is the "greatest commandment" (Mk 12:28). Love is the origin of the historical event of man's redemption in Christ (see Gal 2:20; Eph 5:2, 25).

4. *Man experiences divine sonship.* In Christianity man rediscovers his true vocation, which is to become a son of God. The

mystery of the Father also leaves its mark on the "economy" (the successive stages of the history of salvation), which involves the reintegration of the whole of humanity into his kingdom in order to make men sons in the Son. This is why he sent his Son (see Jn 3:16; Gal 4:4; Rom 8:3). Jesus' message shows that God is the Father of all (Mt 5:45; Lk 6:35), above all of the disinherited and the sinners (see the parable of the prodigal son in Lk 15:1–32). Hence the very timely thought of the radical brotherhood of all men. Adoption as sons of God in the Son is a Christian privilege that all are invited to receive. This is the source of the Christian civilization of love and equality.

5. *Christian existence is an experience of meeting Christ the savior in the ecclesial community.* In Christianity man does not remain alone to carry out his ascetical endeavors, but is sustained by the ecclesial community. The Church is not just an environment for social relations, but an ambit of salvation, joy, hope, and solidarity. By means of the sacraments man's human and spiritual maturation is reinforced. The Church is essentially an integral experience of salvation: it is the hope of eternal life, but also an existence set free from anguish, solitude, desperation, and meaninglessness.

The salvation we are talking about here is one that has already been realized in partial and provisional ways in history. At the same time, it enlightens and upholds man's existence on the way to an authentic fulfillment of all of his human possibilities (meaning for life, freedom, communion with others), as well as concretely transforms situations of injustice, unfreedom, slavery, need, poverty, and underdevelopment of persons and communities.

Christian salvation concerns man in his entirety, whether as an individual or as communion with others. It is a present to be lived and realized, as well as a future to hope for and to enjoy fully. It is cosmic, inasmuch as even nature shares in man's salvation and will attain its fulfillment at the end of times together with all humankind. Christian salvation remains open, in the sense that, because Christ and his Church are universal sacraments of salvation for humanity, this salvation remains fundamentally available to all.

Chapter 9

The Meaning of Salvation in Jesus Christ Today

There are essentially four principal aspects of Christian salvation:

1. the experience of personal communion with Christ (the personal dimension);

2. the experience of communion in the Church (the dimension of the Church);

3. the experience of a re-created existence (the dimension of salvation);

4. the experience of authentic orthopraxy (the practical-cultural dimension).

The Personal Dimension: Rediscovering Baptism

The Harmony between Knowledge and Faith Experience

The cognitive horizon that we have been setting forth in the previous chapters is a well-founded, solid basis for a convinced and dynamic experience of Christian life. Jesus is truth, but he is also the way and the life (see Jn 14:6). The Christian tradition sees a harmony between orthodoxy and orthopraxy, between the right profession of faith and its enactment in concrete deeds: "Firm and well-pondered convictions are an impulse to courageous and right action" (CT, 22). "Being Christian" is not exclusively a matter of understanding the mystery of Christ without a corresponding experience of faith and life in him. The Christian's mature knowledge of Jesus has to become "pneumatic" existence in him. In this way, it will give the Christian's

121

life the dimension of a committed pilgrimage of faith, hope, and charity.

The first experiential criterion that emerges from the narration of the story of Jesus is that of personal encounter with him. The narrative of Jesus' story becomes the story of every Christian's life with him today. Like the first disciples, who were called and followed under the action of the Holy Spirit, Christians today are immersed in the divine life of the Trinity through baptism. That is, Christians are called by name, not only to knowledge, but to an existence of faith and sonship in the Spirit of the risen Christ.

It is a matter of recognizing Jesus experientially as a faithful friend, as a model of human realization, and as a teacher of fraternal life. Above all, and even more radically, it is a matter of recognizing and experiencing Jesus as the Messiah and savior of one's own personal existence: "We have found the Messiah (which means Christ)" (Jn 1:41). These are Andrew's words to his brother Simon after having met and known Jesus. In baptism, Jesus' history becomes the history of the disciples and of every Christian. Consequently, Christian life becomes life "of Christ, in Christ, for Christ, toward Christ." Christ becomes the center of the personal history of every one of his disciples.

This dimension of the personal experience of Christ is a wonderfully original part of Christian existence, especially when we compare it with other, non-Christian models of religious life. Intrinsic relation to Jesus Christ does not spell the death of each person's human identity, but exalts and strengthens it.

Let us reread the dialogue between Jesus and his first disciples as the Evangelist John tells it (he even notes the hour of the meeting):

> The two disciples heard him saying this, and they followed Jesus. Jesus turned and saw them following, and said to them, "What do you seek?" And they said to him, "Rabbi" (which means teacher), "where are you staying?" He said to them, "Come and see." They came and saw where he was staying; and they stayed with him that day, for it was about the tenth hour. (Jn 1:37–39)

The disciples stayed with him not only on the day that he called them, but for their entire life.

"Abide in My Love" (Jn 15:9)

During his earthly existence, Jesus called his disciples to "live" with him. He invited them to "follow him," to "imitate him," to be in full "communion" with him, and to "share" together with him in prayer, the apostolate, and the sacrifice of the cross. We find this experience thematized in the Gospels, especially the Gospel of John, as well as in the letters of Paul. Jesus compares himself to the vine and his disciples to the branches:

> Abide in me, and I in you. As the branch cannot bear fruit by itself, unless it abides in the vine, neither can you, unless you abide in me. I am the vine, you are the branches. He who abides in me, and I in him, he it is that bears much fruit, for apart from me you can do nothing.... Abide in my love. (Jn 15:4–9)

Without communion with Jesus, there is neither apostolate nor participation in God's trinitarian life. The Eucharist is the sacrament of communion with Jesus on earth: "He who eats my flesh and drinks my blood abides in me, and I in him. As the living Father sent me, and I live because of the Father, so he who eats me will live because of me" (Jn 6:55–56). Communion with Jesus is communion with the Father: "I am in my Father, and you in me, and I in you" (Jn 14:20).

"For Me to Live Is Christ" (Phil 1:21)

In preparation for the Jubilee of the Year 2000, Pope John Paul II invites us to "rediscover baptism as the foundation of Christian existence, according to the words of the Apostle: 'as many of you as were baptized into Christ have put on Christ' (Gal 3:27)" (TMA, 41).

It is a good time to meditate again on what Saint Paul experienced in this area, transmitting to the Church one of the most successful experiences of life and mission lived entirely in and for Christ. This is a basic spiritual experience which can be expressed with a variety of terms such as "communion," "divinization," "participation," "conformation," "assimilation," and "incorporation."

Saint Paul's life was a never-ending assimilation to Christ: "For me to live is Christ" (Phil 1:21). When Paul was converted on the road to Damascus (Acts 9:3–5; 22:1–12; 26:1–24), Jesus revealed himself to be present and living in the Church and in Christians: "I am Jesus whom you are persecuting" (Acts 9:5).

Paul describes this vital assimilation to Christ and the sharing of Christ's life with neologisms like "co-death" and "co-life" with Christ (2 Tim 2:11; Rom 6:8), "co-suffering" (Rom 8:17; 1 Cor 12:26), "being co-crucified" (Rom 6:6), "being co-buried" (Rom 6:4; Col 2:12), "to co-resurrect" (Eph 2:6; Col 2:18; 3:1), "to be con-figured" to Christ in death (Phil 3:10), to be "con-glorified" (Rom 8:17), "to co-sit" (Eph 2:6) and "co-reign" with him (2 Tim 2:12; 1 Cor 4:8), to be "co-heirs" (Rom 8:17; Eph 3:6). Christians, in other words, have been predestined by the Father "to be con-formed to the image of his Son" (Rom 8:29).

The reality of the baptized person is his incorporation into Christ:

> But God, who is rich in mercy, out of the great love with which he loved us, even when we were dead through our trespasses, made us alive together with [co-vivified us] Christ (by grace you have been saved), and raised us up with him [co-raised us], and made us sit in the heavenly places [co-seated us] in Christ Jesus, that in the coming ages he might show the immeasurable riches of his grace in kindness toward us in Christ Jesus. (Eph 2:4–7)

The Apostle uses many images to describe how the baptized are united with Christ: "You are God's field, God's building (1 Cor 3:9); "Do you not know that you are God's temple, and that God's Spirit dwells in you? If anyone destroys God's temple, God will destroy him. For God's temple is holy, and that temple you are" (1 Cor 3:16–17).

There are more personalistic images: "You are fellow citizens with the saints and members of the household of God, built on the foundation of the apostles and prophets, Christ Jesus being the cornerstone" (Eph 2:19–20); "I feel a divine jealousy for you, for I betrothed you to Christ to present you as a pure bride to her one husband" (2 Cor 11:2). The analogy of spousal communion expresses well the Christian's intimate communion with Jesus: "Do you not know that your bodies are members of Christ? Shall I therefore take the members of Christ and make them members of a prostitute? Never!...But he who is united to the Lord becomes one spirit with him" (1 Cor 6:15–17; see Eph 5:21–32).

The Pauline analogy par excellence is that of the "mystical body." In baptism, believers have become "the body of Christ and individually members of it" (1 Cor 12:27): "For as in one body we have many members, and all the members do not have the same function, so we, though many, are one body in Christ, and individually members one of another" (Rom 12:4–5); "Rather, speaking the truth in love, we are to grow up in every way into him who is the head, into Christ, from whom the whole body, joined and knit together by every joint with which it is supplied, when each part is working properly, makes bodily growth and upbuilds itself in love" (Eph 4:15–16). The image of the mystical body is the best expression of the believer's lived participation in the saving mystery of Christ, a participation by which he becomes one with Christ: "You are all one in Christ Jesus" (Gal 3:28). This experience is one of a life of total assimilation to Christ: "I have been crucified with Christ; it is no longer I who live, but Christ lives in me" (Gal 2:20); "For me to live is Christ" (Phil 1:21); Christ is "our life" (Col 3:3).

The Trinitarian Dimension of Incorporation into Christ

Incorporation into Christ brings the believer into relation with the Persons of the Trinity and, at the same time, establishes a new relationship with men. This union makes Christians adopted children of the Father: "Blessed be the God and Father of our Lord Jesus Christ, who has blessed us in Christ with every spiritual blessing in the heavenly places, even as he chose us in him before the foundation of the world, that we should be holy and blameless before him. He destined us in love to be his sons through Jesus Christ, according to the purpose of his will" (Eph 1:3–5). The adoption meant here is not extrinsic and juridical, but conforms and assimilates us as sons to Christ: "For those whom he foreknew he also predestined to be conformed to the image of his Son" (Rom 8:29); "For you did not receive a spirit of slavery to fall back into fear, but you have received the spirit of sonship. When we cry 'Abba! Father!' it is the Spirit himself bearing witness with our spirit that we are children of God, and if children, then heirs, heirs of God and fellow heirs with Christ, provided we suffer with him in order that we may also be glorified with him" (Rom 8:15–17).

United with Christ, the baptized do not form a shapeless jumble of closed individual existences, but a living organism full of interconnections. Every believer not only has an intrinsic relation of his own to Christ, the head of the mystical body, but also an original function and interrelation with the other members: "But grace was given to each of us according to the measure of Christ's gift" (Eph 4:7). Inserted into the communion of trinitarian life, Christians live in union, communion, and sharing of goods (since all are coheirs), independently of nation, race, social condition, and sex (see Gal 3:28).

The Plurality of Experiences of Communion with Christ

This christological spirituality — which we live in prayer and the sacraments, in listening to the Word of God, in serving our neighbor, and in the communion of the Church — is basically one and the same for all, inasmuch as it is a life of sonship in the Trinity. Nevertheless, in the concrete each person lives this experience differently. Cyril of Jerusalem likens God's grace to the dew which on the lily is white, on the rose pink, and purple on violets and hyacinths. The dew takes on different colors according to the different kinds of things; the dew on the palm is different from the dew on the vine. Nevertheless, it is always the same water that gives life and beauty to the multiform world (*Catechesis,* 16, 12). Consequently, the history of the Church has known a great variety of experiences of the soul's assimilation to God.

This experience was the goal of Eastern and Western monasticism. In both cases, monasticism is characterized by the striving for holiness through radical asceticism, which in turn lays the groundwork for mystical experience and the ever greater expansion of the Spirit in the soul.

The dominant element in Russian mysticism, for example, is total estrangement from the world and complete dedication to contemplation and self-abandonment in God through prayer. This prayer is "prayer of the heart," which becomes existential communion with God, the breath of the Holy Spirit in the soul, and thus a verification in one's own life of the word of God: "I slept, but my heart was awake" (Song 5:2). The Russian pilgrim makes prayer of the heart so much a part of his life that it is almost as if he assimilates it physically: "After some time, I felt—I don't know how—that the prayer went by itself from the lips to the heart. What I mean is that my heart, with its regular beat, began in a certain way to set the pace by itself for the words of the prayer" (*Tales of a Russian Pilgrim*, second account). The prayer ceases to be an action, an effort, and becomes a state and a consolation. It is so present and vibrant that one morning it is the prayer that awakens the pilgrim, comforts him, and sustains him.

Western Christianity also has an abundance of autobiographical works written by great saints and mystics who describe with matchless spiritual delicacy their personal path of perfection and loving communion with Jesus. For example, in the *Dialogue of Divine Providence,* dictated by Catherine of Siena in the fall of 1378, we find an account of her assimilation to Christ the mediator and "bridge." There are other examples: the total commitment to asceticism and mysticism celebrated by the *Spiritual Exercises* written by Saint Ignatius of Loyola between 1522 and 1548; the rediscovery of lost interiority in Teresa of Avila's *Interior Castle* (1577); the experience of union with Jesus described by John of the Cross in the *Spiritual Canticle* (1584), as well as in two works from almost the same period: the *Ascent of Mount Carmel* and the *Dark Night;* Thérèse of the Child Jesus' story of her ardent assimilation to the passion of Christ in *The Story of a Soul* (1895–97).

We have cited only a few examples from among those who

have written down their experience. In addition to such people, there is a multitude of men and women of every age, class, condition, and race whose communion with God is a wonderful secret between God and their soul and who let out only the perfume of their humility and the flavor of their virtue. The Christian who is united and conformed to Christ is the most credible proclamation of Jesus: the kindly face of Mother Teresa of Calcutta shows better than any other word the shining countenance of Jesus. The Christian transfigured by the charity of Christ is the best preacher of his saving mystery.

Let us cite a passage taken from the *Life in Christ* of Nicholas Cabasilas (Thessalonika 1319/23–1397/98), which describes the assimilation of souls to Christ through the sacraments:

> The Savior is always totally present in those who live in him: he provides for their every need, he is everything for them, and he does not allow them to turn their eyes to any other object or to seek anything outside of him. In fact, there is nothing that the saints need that is not he: he generates them, makes them grow and nourishes them, and is their light and breath; he shapes their vision through himself, illuminates them by means of himself, and in the end presents themselves to their eyes. He both feeds and is their food; it is he who offers them the bread of life, and what he offers is himself; the life of the living, the perfume of those who breathe, the garment for whoever wants to wear him. He also is the one who enables us to walk and is our life, as well as the place of rest and the goal. We are the members and he is the head: is it necessary to fight? he fights with us and it is he who awards victory to him who has acquitted himself honorably. Are we victorious? Lo, he is the crown. He thus leads our mind back to himself from every side and does not allow it to turn to anything else or to be seized with love for anything else.... From what we have said it is clear that life in Christ does not concern only the future, but is present already now for the saints who live and work in it. (*The Life in Christ*, I, 13–15)

Option for Christ and Bearing Witness

There are other experiences that deserve a fresh look from the pastoral point of view inasmuch as they realize the personal experience of the baptized person in Christ. These are the Christian's fundamental option and his witness.

To follow Christ is to choose him as the master who teaches us how to live. To choose Jesus means to "be with him" (Mk 3:14), to "follow him wherever" he goes (Lk 9:47–62), to go "after him" (Mk 1:17). It means to bring one's life into harmony with the very life of Jesus, to the point of "carrying the cross" that he has carried (Mk 8:34) (VS, 6–27).

The following of Jesus Christ becomes a fundamental option (see VS, 65–70) when the experience of Christ orients the Christian's practical action, moving him to labor day by day to bring into harmony what he believes in faith and his action. The point, then, is choosing Christ as the goal that orients, illumines, and guides by his grace the often hesitant steps of the Christian's free decisions. The fundamental option is to accept "being authentically Christian" as a way of life that determines and orients the believer's historical path in every one of his free actions. It is thus to live "with Jesus," according to "Jesus' standards," hence, according to faith, hope, and charity, and not according to the standards of egoism, usefulness, and naked rationality.

The Christian's fundamental option is not a single choice made solemnly in the past. Rather, it is a habitual direction of the Christian's path thanks to the enlightenment and support of the grace of Christ. This option has to be recognizable as such in every single concrete choice. The fundamental option can be called christocentric when, choosing Jesus as the absolute good, we do concrete and particular acts in harmony with this absolute good. This gives rise to a real direction toward the good.

Here is the foundation of the testimony of the baptized (see VS, 89–94; 137–38; 181–82), who becomes by his existence and action a witness to Christ, to the point of giving his own life for Christ in the supreme surrender of martyrdom.

The "Ecclesial Dimension"

Life in Christ Is the Experience of Ecclesial Communion

What the Christian lives in his own person has an intrinsic communitarian aspect. His encounter with Jesus in baptism takes place in the context of the ecclesial community and is thus an encounter with the community of faith, hope, and charity that is expressed and celebrated in a special and privileged way in the liturgy of the Eucharist. In the Eucharist, the baptized live together their experience of salvation in the mystery of Christ's Passover. To live with Jesus is thus to live with the Church and in the Church.

In the Church our personal encounter with him becomes a sacramental encounter and thus a bestowal of grace and redemption.

Some ways to realize and bring to maturity this ecclesial experience are:

a. the liturgy and the life of prayer;

b. an attitude of ecclesial communion formed by obedience, collaboration, readiness to serve all the levels and grades and components of the body of Christ which is the Church. For it is Christ who is the center, the support, and the accomplisher of the Church's unity;

c. the "associative" life (ecclesial movements), as a locus of experience and of community commitment, of maturation of faith, and of human solidarity.

The prayer that Jesus taught — the "Our Father" — obliges Christians to be in communion with each and every human person, for all of them are called to be sons and daughters of God in Christ. There is thus an intrinsic demand for universal brotherhood under the merciful eyes of the Father. Accordingly, the Christian does not discriminate against anyone for any reason (be it difference of religion, race, sex, or social standing).

This lived experience of the Church is the legitimation of every Christian movement, group, or association. We live our personal experience of following Jesus Christ together with that of other brothers and sisters; in this way, our experience becomes ecclesial. It becomes the discernment and the vibrant sharing of charisms and personal gifts (see 1 Cor 12–14) which are made available for the use and edification of one's own sanctification, as well as for the sanctification of the ecclesial community in an authentic life of charity (1 Cor 13).

One privileged experience of Christ in the context of the community that has known a vibrant plurality of forms, capacity for renewal, and perennial timeliness throughout history is the "consecrated life." The vocation to the consecrated life is by its nature a personal and communal experience of Christ: it is life in Christ and in the Church in a particular apostolic mission in the world.

"Lord, Teach Us to Pray" (Lk 11:1)

It is useful to rediscover Christian prayer today by contemplating the icon of Jesus in prayer. This is a fascinating side of Jesus' personality that has created an authentic, millennial tradition of Christian spirituality and holiness that is waiting to be rediscovered and to be made the most of. Jesus' originality in this field has been grasped even by non-Christians, who see in him not only a pious Jew, but above all an unsurpassable master of spiritual life and intimacy with God.

The disciples, who themselves were experts in the Jewish prayer of their time, were so struck by the uniqueness of their master's prayer that they asked him, "Lord, teach us to pray" (Lk 11:1). That Jesus' prayed is one of the best documented aspects of the historical Jesus. He prayed in the morning: "And in the morning, a great while before day, he rose and went out to a lonely place, and there he prayed" (Mk 1:35). He prayed in the evenings: after the multiplication of the loaves, he "dismissed the crowds, [and] went up into the hills by himself to pray. When evening came, he was there alone" (Mt 14:23). He prayed at night time: before choosing the twelve Apostles, Jesus "went out into the hills to pray; and all night he continued in prayer to God" (Lk 6:12). Jesus prayed without ceasing: "he withdrew to the wilderness and prayed" (Lk 5:16).

The most important moments of Jesus' life are accompanied by prayer: Jesus prays at his baptism in the Jordan (Lk 3:21); he prays before calling the Apostles (Lk 6:12); he prays before the transfiguration (Lk 9:28); he prays for Peter's faith (Lk 22:31–32); he prays for the sending of the Holy Spirit (Jn 14:15–17a); he prays before raising Lazarus (Jn 11:41); he prays at the time of his triumphal entry into Jerusalem (Jn 12:27); he prays to the Father during the Last Supper that he, Jesus, might be glorified (Jn 17:1–5); he prays for his disciples (Jn 17:6–19) and for all believers (Jn 17:20–26); he prays before his passion (Lk 22:39, 46); while being crucified he prays for his executioners (Lk 23:34) and when he dies he prays with confidence to the Father (Lk 23:46).

In his prayer Jesus does follow less the official time of Jewish prayer than the rhythm of the proclamation of the kingdom and of the realization in history of his event of salvation. This is the new time of Christian prayer which substitutes the old time of the Jewish tradition. It is no longer a chronological time, but an entirely christological time of salvation.

Jesus adds to his words outward gestures like kneeling (Lk 22:41) or raising his eyes to heaven (Mt 14:19; Jn 11:41; 17:1; see Ps 123:1). Jesus prays above all in silence, but contemplating the Father. Although he knows the official prayer (see the prayers said during the Passover meal: Mk 14:20; Mt 26:30), he prefers personal, spontaneous prayer. He does not pray like the good Pharisees of his time who stood in the synagogues or on the street corners in order to be seen by men (Mt 6:5). He prays to the Father in secret (see Mt 6:6) and very often alone, even when he is with the disciples.

In this connection, Luke gives us a singular oxymoron when he says that "it happened that as he was praying alone while the disciples were with him, he asked them this question" (Lk 9:18). This episode prefigures in a certain sense the solitude that Jesus experiences in his heart in Gethsemani despite being accompanied by his disciples. As the Venerable Bede observes, "Nowhere — unless I am mistaken — is it said that he prayed with the disciples. Instead, he prays everywhere alone, because man's desires cannot understand God's design; no one can become a partaker of this interior mystery together with Christ" (*In Lucae Evangelium Expositio,* III).

The Father: Horizon of Jesus' Prayer

The mountain or desert where Jesus prays is the silence of God. His prayer is tied less to a place — such as the temple in Jerusalem or a synagogue — than to a person, namely, the Father. The temple in which he prays is his union with the Father. Prayer thus has an important interior dimension that is not correlative to set rituals or fixed times, but to the unfolding of his saving event. It is the person of Jesus himself — his action, his attitude, his words — that constitutes the other pole of prayer in addition to the Father. Therefore, prayer is not an interval of distraction or rest, but an unbroken dialogue with the Father in order to strengthen his resolve to obey his mission: "Sacrifices and offerings thou hast not desired, but a body thou hast prepared for me.... Then I said, 'Lo, I have come to do thy will, O God' " (Heb 10:5–7). "My food is to do the will of him who sent me and to accomplish his work" (Jn 4:34; see also Jn 5:30; 6:38; 8:29; 8:55; 9:4).

Obedience to the Father's will is also at the center of the dramatic prayer in the garden of Gethsemani (see, Lk 22:39–46; Mt 26:36–46; Mk 14:32–42). In this prayer, the Son, through his human will that is tragically tested by sufferings and pain, confirms his oblation to the Father (see Heb 5:7–10).

Jesus' union with the Father is not an ascetical effort, but a reality in which he lives and in which he rejoices beyond measure: "I thank thee, Father, Lord of heaven and earth.... All things have been delivered to me by my Father; and no one knows the Son except the Father, and no one knows the Father except the Son and anyone to whom the Son chooses to reveal him" (Mt 11:25, 27).

Thus, it is when Jesus prays that we can grasp his true identity as "the Christ of God" (Lk 9:20), an identity that his disciples and adversaries continually mistake and deny. The same Luke, immediately after the episode of Peter's confession, relates the event of the transfiguration, which also occurs during prayer: "Now about eight days after these sayings he took with him Peter and John and James, and went up on the mountain to pray. And as he was praying, the appearance of his countenance was altered, and his raiment became dazzling white" (Lk 9:28–29). Here, too, it is during prayer that Jesus reveals his true countenance: he is the "Son," the "Chosen" (Lk 9:35).

Prayer enables the incarnate Word to remain with the Father, to be turned continually toward him and wholly gathered in his bosom. Although he came to dwell in our midst, Jesus never distanced himself from communion with the Father in prayer. Inasmuch as his prayer was a continual act of filial obedience — "not my will, but thine be done" (Lk 22:42) — it is also the basis of his mission. Being with God does not mean to withdraw from the brethren, but to be with them with the very goodness, mercy, and condescension of the Father. Intimacy with the Father becomes a saving and merciful closeness to the neighbor to the point of the supreme sacrifice.

By his prayer Jesus shows that he did not merely preach and practice an ethical or social gospel, but also lived an intense spiritual life. Indeed, this rooting in the Father's heart was the source of his apostolic dynamism. This is one of the aspects that Christian pastoral ministry most has to recover today. What is needed is a renewed understanding of prayer as interiority, as the horizon of a unified life, and as the true realization of our humanity.

The Experience of Salvation

The lived experience that is at once christocentric, personal, and communitarian is also of its very nature an experience of integral salvation. In fact, life in Christ and the Church offers not only enlightenment and knowledge, but also the help and the strength we need to overcome the spiritual, moral, and physical limits of our unsaved, meaningless existence. The key to success in the Christian life is this experience of lived salvation. The recognition that Jesus is the savior of all people implies the well-grounded awareness that our existence in faith is an existence that is not only filled with sense and meaning, but is also saved.

Typical moments where this experience of salvation is verified and expressed are, among others, so-called conversions, whether in the sense of a radical change of one's fundamental option in favor of Christ, or in the sense of partial correction and improvement of one's life of faith.

This pastoral context gives rise to the need for correctly instructing the Christian in the sacrament of reconciliation, which must be seen less as a mere comprehensive renewal of one's life of faith than as a gradual process of healing whose highest and most efficacious celebration is found in the sacramental pardon imparted in absolution. This is the so-called therapeutic dimension of the sacrament of reconciliation, which joins to sacramental pardon a correct pedagogy designed to strengthen or restore those virtuous habits weakened or even destroyed by sin.

In this context, the significance of penance becomes that of the ethical maturation of the Christian, who passes gradually from a state of spiritual sickness and injury to a state of spiritual healing and health. This work of spiritual and moral reconstruction is accomplished through the pastoral ministry of confessors, who are not only judges, but are above all spiritual fathers, physicians of souls, and wise teachers of their penitents.

Associated as they are with the saving mystery of Jesus' death and resurrection, Christians know that in him they are a new humanity. They are, in other words, liberated and liberating; they are dynamically open to overcoming all obtuseness and falsehood in order to live their message of the kingdom as a proposal of peace and universal brotherhood, of the defence of life in all its aspects, and of respect for nature and the cosmos.

In Jesus, the land of the living, Christians plan and carry out the continual renewal of their history as persons and as a community. Mission is itself the urgency of proclaiming and sharing with all the nations the Christian experience of salvation (see Mt 28:19–20). At the summit of this lived salvation is the experience of "Christian spirituality" as life in Christ and his Spirit of charity.

The "Practical-Cultural" Dimension of Experience

Experience of Faith and Christian Praxis

The experience of salvation in Christ impels the Christian ineluctably to action, testimony, mission, and dialogue. Christian orthodoxy becomes not only the lived experience of persons and the community, but also personal and social praxis.

The Christ whom we celebrate and live becomes human time and space, history and culture, language and attitudes, tradition and development. The religious life of Christians becomes cultural synthesis. A new culture arises that is capable of leavening and transforming other human and religious cultures into the civilization of love.

In and through Christians, the history of Christ becomes a culture and life of salvation. This culture does not reject anything that is authentically human and religious, because it is the realization and fulfillment of every human and religious utopia. This culture, like the life of Christians itself, is not a static, but a dynamic reality. It is already in act, but in a continual phase of realization and fulfillment.

We have here the peak of the practical and cultural relevance of the proclamation of Christ. Therefore, Christian culture spurs human history to transcend continually its own limits and its own dark sides until reaching its final fulfillment in him.

The various currents of liberation theology, the valid orientations of the Church's social teaching, and even political projects of Christian inspiration all express — albeit with diverse emphases — this demand for practical inculturation of the faith in today's world.

Let us suggest a few themes — themes with educational value — for this christocentric pastoral effort. Such themes could be the truth, freedom, dignity, value, and equality of every human person; universal brotherhood, the inviolability of life, respect for and defense of nature, world peace, just distribution of the world's goods, protection of the rights of the handicapped and of minors. These are all areas for christological praxis and inculturation.

By means of Christian praxis, the mystery of Christ thus becomes a gift of salvation for all.

The Culture of Hope

One of the most dismal and disquieting aspects of today's culture, above all in the West, is its lack of hope. Humankind seems to have plunged into anguish and fear about its own survival. The reasons are numerous: unjust wars, divisions among peoples, the use of ever more powerful weapons, the almost irreversible poverty of entire continents, the diminishment of concern for solidarity with the needy and the weak, growing unemployment, the standardization of culture, ecological imbalances caused by often imprudent and violent interferences with nature, contagious diseases spread in perverse ways, and increasingly widespread drug use among young people. The international scientific world is witnessing the multiplication of journals devoted to "suicidology," the science of suicide — the supreme act of solitude and mistrust of life. The "postmodern" horizon seems to be turning man's existence into a Dantean hell: "Abandon all hope, ye that enter here" (*Inf.*, III, 9).

Sociologists divide the indices of hopelessness into cultural and structural signs. The *cultural signs* include the consequences of the complexity of society. Examples are: the crisis of the "we" and the loss of solidarity, extreme forms of pluralism, heightened consumerism, the crisis of confidence in the future and in welcoming life — which is seen more as a threat than as an enrichment of one's own existence — the culture of pleasure, esotericism, and the crisis of speech.

Structural signs include the aging of the population of the so-called "first world," economic poverty, unemployment, especially among the young, and the crisis of the nuclear family.

It is perhaps not out of place to mention here scholarly analyses that can help restore confidence to humanity. Philosophers and theologians have zeroed in on hope as the key to interpreting the meaning of man's life. Not desperation or fear, but hope, is the ontological structure that accounts for the progress of history toward new things and which grounds the possibility of every one of man's free actions and decisions.

For Christians, the "principle of hope" is the person of Jesus Christ and his message. Jesus Christ is the one who gives man's hope its ultimate meaning in two limit situations — death and history. In the face of death, the Christian knows that he is not on the path to nothingness, but to an existence full of happiness in God. In the face of history, the Christian is taught to read in the often apocalyptic chaos of historical events a plot of life leading to salvation.

The Holy Father John Paul II has become the great prophet of Christian hope in today's world. His apostolic voyages in a hundred nations of the earth are messages proclaiming the hope not only of eternal life, but also of a liberated and authentically human existence. They recall us to peace, justice, brotherhood, solidarity, acceptance, equality, freedom, and the defense of the little ones, the marginalized, the poor, and the outcasts: "Have no fear of that which you yourselves have created, have no fear of all that man has produced, and that every day is becoming more dangerous for him! Finally, have no fear of yourselves" (*CTH,* 219)

Why must we not be afraid? Because man has been redeemed by Christ and the grace of the resurrection is the surplus value that pervades the history of humanity. The power of Jesus' cross and resurrection is stronger than any evil that man could and should fear.

The Pope continues:

"Be not afraid" Christ said to the Apostles (see Lk 24:36) and the women (see Mt 28:10) after the Resurrection.... Peoples and nations of the entire world need to hear these words. *Their conscience needs to grow in the certainty that Someone exists who holds in His hands the destiny of this passing world, Someone who holds the keys to death and the netherworld* (see Rev 1:18); *Someone who is the Alpha and the Omega of human history* (see Rev 22:18) — be it the individual or collective history. And this Someone is Love (see 1 Jn 4:8, 16) — Love that became man, Love crucified and risen, Love unceasingly present among men. It is Eucharistic love. It is the infinite source of communion. He alone can give the ultimate assurance when He says, "Be not afraid." (*CTH*, 220-22.)

Christians are invited not only to perform gestures of hope, but also to make the most of the signs of hope present in today's world:

> Moreover, it is necessary to turn to account and to deepen the signs of hope present at century's end, notwithstanding the shadows that often conceal them from our eyes. In civil society, such signs are the progress that has been made by science, technology, and especially medicine in serving human life; the keener sense of responsibility toward the environment; the efforts to reestablish peace and justice wherever they have been violated; the resolute desire for reconciliation and solidarity among peoples, especially in the complex relations between the North and South of the world.... In the Church, such signs are more attentive listening to the voice of the Spirit through the acceptance of charisms and the promotion of the laity; intense devotion to the cause of unity on the part of individual Christians; the space given to dialogue with the religions and with contemporary culture." (*TMA*, 46)

The Culture of Life

To live in hope is to welcome, defend, protect, and give life. In a world that seems to despise, reject, humiliate, and kill life, the Christian is called to a new proclamation of Jesus Christ, "the Word of life" (1 Jn 1:1), and his "Gospel of Life." This "*Gospel of Life* is not a simple reflection, even though original and profound, on human life; nor is it only a commandment for the sake of sensitizing consciences and causing changes in society; much less is it an illusory promise of a better future. The *Gospel of Life* is a concrete and personal reality, for it consists in the proclamation of the very person of Jesus" (*EV*, 29).

In his inspired prophetic vision, John Paul II looks to the cosmic Christ as the good news of life for all humankind. In the city of man, whose entire existence is menaced by the evil specter of death, the Pope aims to plant the tree of life which is Jesus Christ and his mystery of salvation: "The *Gospel of Life* is not exclusively for believers: it is for all.... The *Gospel of Life* is for the city of men" (*EV*, 101). Not only Christians, but all of the humanity created by God and saved by the cross of the Son of God must feed on the fruits of the tree of life.

The Pope seems to be referring to the Johannine vision of the world as an immense vineyard, in which Jesus is the vinestock and humankind is the branches: "Abide in me, and I in you.... I am the vine, you are the branches. He who abides in me, and I in him, he it is that bears much fruit, for apart from me you can do nothing" (Jn 15:4–5). The celebration of life breaks forth from the *lignum vitae* (tree of life) — as the people of the Middle Ages called the cross — placed at the center of human history, which, after its dramatic beginning under the tree of paradise (see Gn 3:24), finds its glorious fulfillment in "the tree of life" in the heavenly Jerusalem: "Also, on either side of the river, the tree of life with its twelve kinds of fruit, yielding its fruit each month; and the leaves of the tree were for the healing of the nations" (Rev 22:2).

In the midst of a scenario of desolation and "apocalyptic" solitude, as our postmodern existence often appears to be, the Christian feels the urgent need for a culture that welcomes life in every form and of an attitude of compassion toward the neediest in order to oppose a culture that is increasingly hardened, pitiless, and cold and that promotes war, tension, hatred, violence, division, and death.

This new Christian culture can make us understand that life is not an egotistic possession, but a gift to welcome with gratitude; that it is not an arbitrary game, but a project of love; that it is not a meaningless accident, but a vocation to be realized; that it is not a problem that is hard to resolve, but a mystery to be contemplated with humility and wonder.

Christian Civilization: "Soul of the World"

There is a very ancient Christian text that expresses well the historical novelty of Christian existence and praxis:

For the distinction between Christians and other men is neither in country nor language nor customs. For they do not dwell in cities in some place of their own, nor do they use any strange variety of dialect, nor practice an extraordinary kind of life. This teaching of theirs has not been discovered by the intellect or thought of busy men, nor are they the advocates of any human doctrine as some men are. Yet while living in Greek and barbarian cities, according as each has obtained his lot, and following the local customs, both in clothing and food and in the rest of life, they show forth the wonderful and confessedly strange character of their citizenship. They dwell in their own fatherlands, but as if sojourners in them; they share all things as citizens, and suffer all things as strangers. Every foreign country is their fatherland, and every fatherland is a foreign country.... Their lot is cast "in the flesh," but they do not live "after the flesh." They pass their time upon the earth, but they have their citizenship in heaven. They obey the appointed laws, and they surpass the laws in their own lives. They love all men and are persecuted by all men.... To put it shortly what the soul is in the body, that the Christians are in the world. The soul is spread through all members of the body, and Christians throughout the cities of the world. The soul dwells in the body, but is not of the body, and Christians dwell in the world, but are not of the world. The soul is invisible, and is guarded in a visible body, and Christians are recognized when they are in the world, but their religion remains invisible. (*The Epistle to Diognetus,* 5, 1–17; 6, 1–4 [*The Apostolic Fathers,* I, Loeb Classical Library, pp. 359–61])

Because of this originality, the Christians of the first centuries called themselves the *tertium genus* (third race), and it is thus that they were apostrophized hostilely by the pagans. The pagans, according to Tertullian, "in the circus often and willingly shouted all together [against the Christians]: how long this *tertium genus? (Scorpiax,* 10, 10).

Tertium genus indicated the place of Christianity in terms of culture and salvation. On the one hand, it went beyond the Jewish tradition and, on the other hand, it was a radical novelty with respect to pagan culture and religion. That is, Christians, though immersed in the culture of their time, lived and constantly created a religious and cultural originality of their own. They created the civilization of love, hope, life, and universal brotherhood.

Every generation of Christians, by means of evangelization and witness, has made an invaluable contribution to the progress of humanity in history and to its eternal salvation. For Christian holiness undeniably has a social and cultural dimension. Holiness contributes to the progress of humankind's path through history. Holiness travels the path of light. The men and women who live their union with God consistently are the men and women who construct the new human community, illuminate it, fill its lacks, bring out its positive potentialities, and sustain it with their works of faith, hope, and charity.

Jesus says: "You are the salt of the earth.... You are the light of the world.... Let your light so shine before men, that they may see your good works and glory to your Father who is in heaven" (Mt 5:13–16).

Chapter 10

Mary, the Mother of Jesus

Mary, Maternal Presence in History

From the very beginning, Mary has been present in the history of Christianity as a mother and protectress, first of Jesus, then of the Church. For this reason, the Christian people turns to her with hope-filled hearts.

Generations of mothers have anxiously entrusted to her maternal protection the future of their children, the happiness and harmony of their families, and the peace of nations. Numberless sick people have implored her intercession for the healing of their bodies and the consolation of their souls. Hosts of poor people have found in prayer to Mary the strength to go on living and hoping: "Hail, holy queen, mother of mercy, our life, our sweetness, our hope."

In the Russian tradition, there is an icon that depicts Mary's mantle covering and protecting the city of Moscow against invaders. The *pokrov*, or mantle, symbolizes her powerful presence over the city. The Blessed Virgin has for centuries — and she continues to do so today — covered all the inhabitants of the cities and villages, their streets, their houses, their work, everything with the mantle of her blessing. She is a motherly presence that is invisible but real. Therefore, every Christian unfailingly turns to her to beg for help, comfort, and consolation in a deep and ongoing dialogue of trustful hearts.

In the Marian hymnography of the very first centuries, there is a hymn for terce which goes like this: "O Mother of God, you are the true virgin who gave the fruit of life.... You, O pure Mother of God, are the hope, protection, and refuge of Christians, an impregnable wall, a calm harbor for the shipwrecked" (*TM* I, 924).

In an ancient *theotókion* (hymn to Mary), she is appealed to as the hope of the world: "O Mother of God, you...showed

143

yourself to be a cherubic throne and have held in your arms the hope of our souls. O best hope of the world, Virgin Mother of God, we beg your powerful protection: have pity on a people gone astray; beg the merciful God to set our souls free from every adversity, O only blessed one" (*TM* I, 929).

A *megalinarion* (hymn pertaining to the *Magnificat*) praises Mary in these terms: "Mother of God, hope of all Christians, protect, defend, and keep all who hope in you" (*TM*, 947).

Mary cannot be absent from the preparation for the great Jubilee of the Year 2000. As the Pope says, "the Holy Virgin... will be present 'transversally,' as it were, throughout the entire preparatory phase" (*TMA*, 43).

Why this reference to Mary? Because she, strong and dynamic woman that she was, is "a model of lived faith" for all believers (see *TMA*, 43).

This reference to Mary is not a superstructure of the Church today, but a reality that is solidly founded upon biblical revelation. Mary is the woman chosen and sanctified by the Trinity to be the Mother of the Son of God and the Mother of the Church.

In a rare mariological passage in the writings of Paul, Mary is placed in a trinitarian context that on the one hand celebrates the charity of the Father, the mission of the Son, and the gift of the Holy Spirit and, on the other hand, the motherly ministry of Mary, the "woman": "But when the time had fully come, God sent forth his Son, born of a woman, born under the law, so that we might receive adoption as sons. And because you are sons, God has sent the Spirit of his Son into our hearts crying, 'Abba! Father!' " (Gal 4:4–5). This passage underscores the essential characteristic of the mystery of Mary whether in theology or in Christian popular piety. The triune God is the original source of salvation. Mary is the woman whom God has chosen to perform the service of being the mother of his Son. This trinitarian relation is the root of the Blessed Virgin Mary's exemplary character, which is declared emblematically by the angel at the Annunciation: "The Lord is with you" (Lk 1:28). Mary is she who is "full of grace" (Lk 1:28), who is "blessed among women" (Lk 1:42), whom all generations will call "blessed" (Lk 1:48). If Christ is the one redeemer and mediator of salvation (see 1 Tim 2:5), Mary is the person who is most perfectly redeemed. In the words of the first Marian text of Vatican II, "in Mary [the Church] admires and extols the loftiest fruit of the redemption and contemplates with joy, as in a spotless image, what she [the Church] desires and hopes to be in her totality" (*SC*, 103). In the Dogmatic Constitution on the Church, the Council again states that "redeemed in an even more sublime way in view of the merits of her Son, [Mary] receives the exalted function and dignity of Mother of God, and thus favorite daughter of the Father and shrine [*sacrarium*] of the Holy Spirit" (*LG*, 53).

Mary, Favored Daughter of the Father

This last affirmation deserves closer examination. Mary is the woman whom the Trinity teaches and sanctifies. In the angel's greeting (see Lk 1:26–28), Mary, as the new "daughter of Zion" (see Zeph 3:14; Joel 2:21; Zech 9:9), becomes the representative of the entire chosen people, the incarnation of the new Israel who welcomes the promise of the Messiah in the name of the whole people. In this way, God dwells in the people once more in Mary, the new ark of the covenant. The Father's choice of Mary rests upon the utter gratuity of his fatherly love. "Full of grace" (Lk 1:28) is a unique title. The Father poured out on her the fullness of his charity and holiness. Mary was filled with grace "a priori," inasmuch as she was chosen to be the mother of the incarnate Son of God.

Down through the centuries, the Church's *sensus fidei* has deepened its meditation on this aspect of Mary's holiness through the dogma of the Immaculate Conception (1854), according to which "the Blessed Virgin Mary, in the first instant of her conception, by a singular grace and privilege of almighty God, in view of the merits of Jesus Christ, the savior of the human race, was preserved from all stain of original sin" (DS, 2803).

The fullness of grace is the index of the excellence and completeness of Mary's holiness and of her special consecration by God. Her response — "behold the handmaid of the Lord; be it done unto me according to thy word" (Lk 1:38) — is an act of full faith and total acceptance of the Father's will. The title "handmaid of the Lord" recalls the mysterious and holy figure in Deutero-Isaiah: the "Ebed YHWH," the meek and innocent man who sacrifices himself for the redemption of others (see Is 40–55). With her "fiat," Mary performs an act of faith that is not only personal, but corporate; she makes it also in the name of the New Israel, which is the Church of Christ. That which Israel was unable to carry out because of its incredulity and disobedience, Mary now accomplishes by her faith and obedience to the Father. Just as the old Israel began with Abraham's act of faith, so too the new Israel begins with Mary's act of faith. While the first woman in the order of creation helped bring about ruin and death, this first woman in the order of redemption helps to bring about salvation and life.

The song of Mary, the Magnificat (Lk 1:46–55), can be called a hymn to the Father, the song of the paternity of God, inasmuch as the mercy of God extends from generation to generation to those who fear him. Contemporary readings of this canticle underscore not only the humility of the handmaid toward God, but also Mary's prophetic role in announcing the work of justice, even human justice, that the advent of the kingdom of God will establish on earth. The almighty Lord, the holy savior, will scatter the proud, cast down the mighty, and send the rich away empty-handed, while he will exalt the humble, fill the hungry with God things, and come to the aid of Israel.

The theme of the Magnificat is basically that the Father loves the humble, the poor, and the oppressed. With her Magnificat, Mary becomes the sign of the Father's mercy toward all. The Magnificat is the canticle of the strong woman who claims the rights of God and man in the face of all the abuses of history.

The relation between God the Father and Mary can be summed up in two titles that are at the basis of her holiness: "daughter" and "spouse." As "daughter" she is full of grace, the first among the redeemed, the first adopted child of the Father. As "spouse," she is associated with the Father in the mystery of the Incarnation of the Son: "When she conceived Christ, gave birth to him, fed him, presented him to the

Father in the temple" (*LG,* 61), Mary cooperated with the Father through obedience, faith, hope, and charity (see *LG,* 55, 56, 63).

The experience of God's fatherhood in Mary reminds every human person of his identity as a *son* or *daughter* of God. To call upon God as a Father is not an alienation or a loss of freedom or a depotentiation of our humanity. Rather, it is the recovery of the authentic face of man and woman, who are created in such close similarity to God and re-created in the Son as sons and daughters of the Father. This is why "there is neither Jew nor Greek, there is neither slave nor free, there is neither male nor female; for you are all one in Christ" (Gal 3:28); "Here there cannot be Greek and Jew, circumcised and uncircumcised, barbarian, Scythian, slave, free man, but Christ is all in all" (Col 3:11).

Consequently, every human being rediscovers his identity as a *brother* or *sister,* son or daughter of a single Father. All are gathered together in the one family of God, all are equally partakers and heir of the kingdom. Hence, Mary is "the great sign with a motherly and merciful face of the closeness of the Father and of Christ, with whom she invites us to enter into communion" (Puebla, 282).

Mary, Mother, Disciple, and Associate of the Son

The most important aspect of the figure of Mary is her intimate union with Jesus as mother — "and Jacob the father of Joseph the husband of Mary, of whom Jesus was born, who is called Christ" (Mt 1:16) — educator, disciple, and cooperator of the "Son of the Most High" (Lk 1:32), the Holy One, the "Son of God" (Lk 1:35). Jesus' humanity is entirely from Mary, just as is his integral human upbringing. She gave her Son her mother's heart, surrounding him with love, care, and respect. Mary brought Jesus up by her work, her motherly devotion, and her commitment to protect him. She educated him with her life, which was poor and serene, industrious and simple, chaste and full of maternal love. She brought him up by her trust in the Father and her willingness to help the needy (her cousin Elizabeth, the spouses at Cana, John). The upbringing the Son received from Mary did not occur in an idyllic situation without uncertainty and conflicts.

Mary's life of union with Christ did not rule out the dramatic character of daily life with its joys and, above all, its sufferings. Indeed, the Holy Family endured persecution, exile, poverty, and even mutual incomprehension (see Lk 2:48–50). In raising the Son, Mary accomplished an authentic pilgrimage of faith, from the birth to the resurrection and Pentecost (see Lk 2:19, 51).

Mary not only educated her divine Son, but was also educated by him in a mysterious way. The following passage from the *Life of Mary* of Maximus the Confessor (580–662 A.D.) is illuminating in this regard:

> The gracious and sweet Lord made his blessed Mother understand the truth: he made her know his true Father; and that she might not consider him to be only a man, but to be God incarnate, he said that the Father's house, the temple, belonged to him, just as everything that is the Father's is also the Son's. They could have taken offense if they had not known this, for they could not attain by themselves the perfect understanding of the truth.... In this place he clearly reminds them for the first time with divine elegance of his true Father, so that they will understand his divinity and know that if God is his Father, it must be that the Son is of the same nature as the Father." (*TM* II, 231).

The same author holds that Christ educated his mother with precepts not of a theoretical nature, but that were founded on the experience of his virtuous behavior:

> These precepts are: the love of God and of men, piety, joviality, sweetness, peace and patience, respect and obedience toward parents, fasting, prayer and every good work. The gracious Lord taught them to men first with deed and then with words. From this moment on, then, holy Mary became the disciple of her sweet Son, the true Mother and

daughter of wisdom, because she did not look upon him any longer in a human way, or as a mere man, but served him with respect as God and received his words as the words of God. (*TM* II, 231)

This is why Mary, in addition to being the mother, is also the disciple of her divine Son: "But he replied to the man who told him, 'Who is my mother, and who are my brethren?' And stretching out his hand toward his disciples, he said, 'Here are my mother and my brethren. For whoever does the will of my Father in heaven is my brother, and sister, and mother" (Mt 12:48–50).

In addition to being mother and disciple, Mary is concretely associated with Christ in a maternal service that is subordinate, dependent, and wholly relative to the mystery of her divine Son. John the Evangelist presents a concrete example of this maternal mediation in the miracle of Cana (Jn 2:1–11).

Here is John Paul II's commentary on this scene:

That Mary takes thought for man's needs means at the same time that she introduces them into the radius of Christ's mission as Messiah and of his saving power. There is thus a mediation. Mary places herself between her Son and men in the reality of their privations, needs, and sufferings. *She places herself "in the middle," that is, she acts as mediatrix, not as an outsider, but in her position as mother,* aware that as such she can — indeed, has the right — to draw her Son's attention to men's needs. Her mediation thus has an intercessory character: Mary "intercedes" for men. (*RM*, 21).

Vatican II and the postconciliar Magisterium have stated more precisely the characteristics of Mary's motherly service (*munus maternum*): this mediation is not necessary, nor does it in any way obscure or substitute or parallel that of Christ, the sole mediator between God and man (see 1 Tim 2:5; see *LG*, 60). Moreover, it is a subordinate (*RM*, 39) and participated mediation, inasmuch as the sole mediation of Christ does not exclude, but rather causes many forms of cooperation in his creatures that comes from divine grace (*RM,* 38).

Mary's mediation, however, is special and extraordinary, and this for two reasons. First, because it is founded upon the divine maternity that is proper to Mary alone (*RM,* 38), as well as upon her fullness of grace, that is, her sanctity (*RM,* 39). In conclusion, as Paul VI had already said, "in the Virgin Mary everything is relative to Christ and everything depends on him: for his sake God the Father chose her from all eternity to be his all-holy mother and honored her with gifts of the Holy Spirit given to no other (*MC,* 25). Mary's mediation has an ecclesiological horizon, inasmuch as Mary, receiving the disciple (see Jn 19:25–27), becomes the mother of her Son's disciples, hence, mother of the Church: "After her Son's departure from this world, her maternity remains in the Church as a maternal mediation: by interceding for all her children, the Mother cooperates with the saving action of her Son, the Redeemer of the world" (*RM,* 40).

In relation to the Father there emerged a spirituality of sonship, of abandonment to the most merciful and tender providence of God. Now, in relation to the Son, there emerged a spirituality of maternity, of welcoming acceptance, of tenderness, of listening, and of service of the Son and the sons. There is a continuity between the two attitudes. Mary, the favorite daughter of the Father, mother of the Son and his disciple and mediatrix, interceded that all may be favorite children of the Father in his Son, Jesus Christ.

Mary, Shrine of the Holy Spirit

The mystery of the Son's Incarnation is wholly under the *virtus pneumatica* of the Holy Spirit. From the Incarnation to Pentecost, the Christ event finds in the Holy Spirit its fundamental dynamism. The sacred writers offer numerous testimonies for the understanding of the relationship between the Holy Spirit and Mary, both in the first chapters of Matthew and Luke and at the beginning of Acts. In Lk 1:35, the angel says to Mary that "the Holy Spirit will come upon you, and the power of the

Most High will overshadow you; therefore the child to be born will be called holy, the Son of God." In Acts 1:14, the same Evangelist, speaking of the Church at Jerusalem in expectation of Pentecost, says, "All these with one accord devoted themselves to prayer, together with the women and Mary the mother of Jesus, and with his brethren." The birth of the Redeemer and the birth of the Church are the work of the Holy Spirit; in both Mary plays her role as mother.

Mary, Model and Teacher of Holiness: Marian Spirituality

The rich teaching of the Bible and theology concerning Mary has encouraged the development of Marian piety in East and West, given rise to dogmatic definitions, produced aspirations to give exemplary Christian witness in the world, and inspired artists and poets to dedicate their masterpieces to the Blessed Virgin. Above all, however, it has given life to a fruitful emulation in holiness, realized through what we can call "Marian spirituality."

In *Redemptoris Mater,* John Paul II has given a powerful synthesis of the Marian spirituality of the icons, especially those of the Eastern tradition:

> They are images that attest to the faith and the spirit of prayer of the good people, which realizes that the Mother of God is present to protect them. In these images, the Virgin shines forth as the image of the divine beauty, the dwelling of eternal Wisdom, the figure of the man of prayer, the prototype of contemplation, the icon of glory. She is shown as the one who even during her earthly life possessed spiritual knowledge inaccessible to human reasonings and thus attained by faith to the most sublime knowledge. (*RM*, 34)

Every period of history and every region of the Church have had a special experience of Mary all its own. This experience finds expression not only in devotion, but also in art, literature, music, liturgy, and theological reflection. Little mission chapels as well as the world's majestic cathedrals — those prodigious flowerings of various architectural styles — are very often dedicated to the Mother of God, who tenderly welcomes her children to guide them to Jesus. This attests to a solid and essential Marian devotion that is theologically connected to Jesus Christ, the savior and redeemer. Mary has, in fact, been present since the beginning in Christian popular piety.

The first liturgical celebrations in her honor date from the Patristic period. Likewise very ancient is the well-known Marian invocation that has been found on a papyrus of the third century: "We take refuge under the protection of thy mercy, Holy Godbearer. Do not ignore our pleas in our need, but save us from danger, O only chaste, only blessed one." Of medieval origin are the "Salve Regina," the "Stabat Mater," the practice of the rosary, and images of the "Lady of the Mantle," who symbolizes protection.

Marian inspiration is a constant element in the lives of the holy founders and foundresses of orders and congregations, both ancient and modern. We see a wonderful variety of names in the women's congregations that take their inspiration from Mary: Servants of Mary, Daughters of Mary, Daughters of Mary Help of Christians, Franciscan Missionaries of Mary, Sisters of the Child Mary, Missionary Sisters of the Immaculata, Minim Sisters of the Sacred Heart of Mary. Contemplating Mary as a shining "real-symbol," the religious families accentuate some aspect of the mystery: the capital event of the Incarnation of the Word, and thus Mary's obedient *fiat;* the episode of the Visitation, hence, her loving, liberating service; the silence of Nazareth, and thus Mary's hiddenness in the busyness of everyday life; the event of the "hour," and therefore Mary's association with Our Lord's passion; the cenacle, hence, ecclesial communion with Mary, mother of the Church. In the constitutions of the orders and congregations, Mary is presented — in some of her most inspired titles — as loving *mother* of her children, *sister* who shares the life and experience of consecration, *teacher* of spirituality, *model* of union with Jesus, *guide* to perfection, resplendent *icon* of the Trinity, *custodian* of Gospel values, *foundress* of the institutes, *patroness* and protectress, continuous and consoling *presence, help* and support, *educator* in the life of faith, hope, and charity, *queen and lady* of consecrated people.

Mary is also a living presence in the various forms of association that animate the Catholic Church. Some movements underscore the spiritual aspect of Christian life: frequent participation in the liturgy and the sacraments, the reading and meditation of the Word of God, interior instruction and formation. Others lay emphasis on the apostolate, on Christian action in the world, on the works of corporal and spiritual mercy. For all, however, Mary has the maternal function of "taking care of the brothers of her Son who are still on pilgrimage and are placed in the midst of dangers and troubles" (*LG,* 62).

While Catholics experience saving communion with Christ in their own lives, they also live an intense devotion to Mary that is inspired and supported by, for example, the example and maternal intercession of the Blessed Virgin. In particular, Mary is seen as the ideal type of the creature as God wanted it in the act of creation, and as a model for man busy about building his temporal and eternal destiny. Mary thus becomes the inspirer of personal, familial, ecclesial, and social involvement, a model of sanctity, of docility to the Word of God and his plan of salvation, of service to family and Church, of welcoming acceptance, of tenderness, of courage, and of strength.

Entrustment to Mary

One form of Marian devotion that is particularly widespread among the Catholic faithful is the so-called consecration, or entrustment, to Mary inspired by Saint Louis M. Grignion de Montfort (see his *Treatise on True Devotion to Mary*). Entrustment, or self-gift, to Mary is a matter of freely and existentially corresponding — in service, prayer, listening, and mission — to God's saving plan. This is a way of making fruitful the consecration already present in us by baptism, the other sacraments, and, in some cases, religious profession. Mary thus becomes the teacher of Christian life.

John Paul II speaks of entrustment to Mary as a biblical reality founded on Jn 19:25–27. Mary's new maternity is included in Jesus' last will and testament on Golgotha: "behold your son." These words indicate the "Marian dimension in the life of Christ's disciples" (*RM*, 45). Mary is entrusted with the disciple and, in him, with all of Jesus' disciples. The disciples are a gift that Jesus makes to Mary: "behold thy mother." "There begins at the foot of the cross that special entrustment of man to the Mother of Christ which since then has been practiced and expressed in various ways in the history of the Church" (*RM*, 45). "Entrustment to Mary is the response to the love of a person, and, in particular, to the love of the mother" (450).

This act has an intrinsically christological meaning: "This filial relationship, this self-entrustment of a son to his mother, not only has its beginning in Christ, but we can say that it is ultimately oriented to him. We can say that Mary continues to repeat to all men the same words that she says at Cana in Galilee: 'Do whatever he tells you' " (*RM*, 46).

John Paul II concludes the encyclical *Evangelium Vitae* (1995) with the following words: "Mary is a living word to console the Church in her struggle against death. By showing us her Son, she assures us that in him the powers of death have already been vanquished: 'Death and life were locked in a wondrous combat. The Lord of life was dead; but now he lives triumphant' " (*EVi*, 105).